Columbus Museum of Art

The Glass Sculpture of Christopher Ries

12 October - 30 December 2001

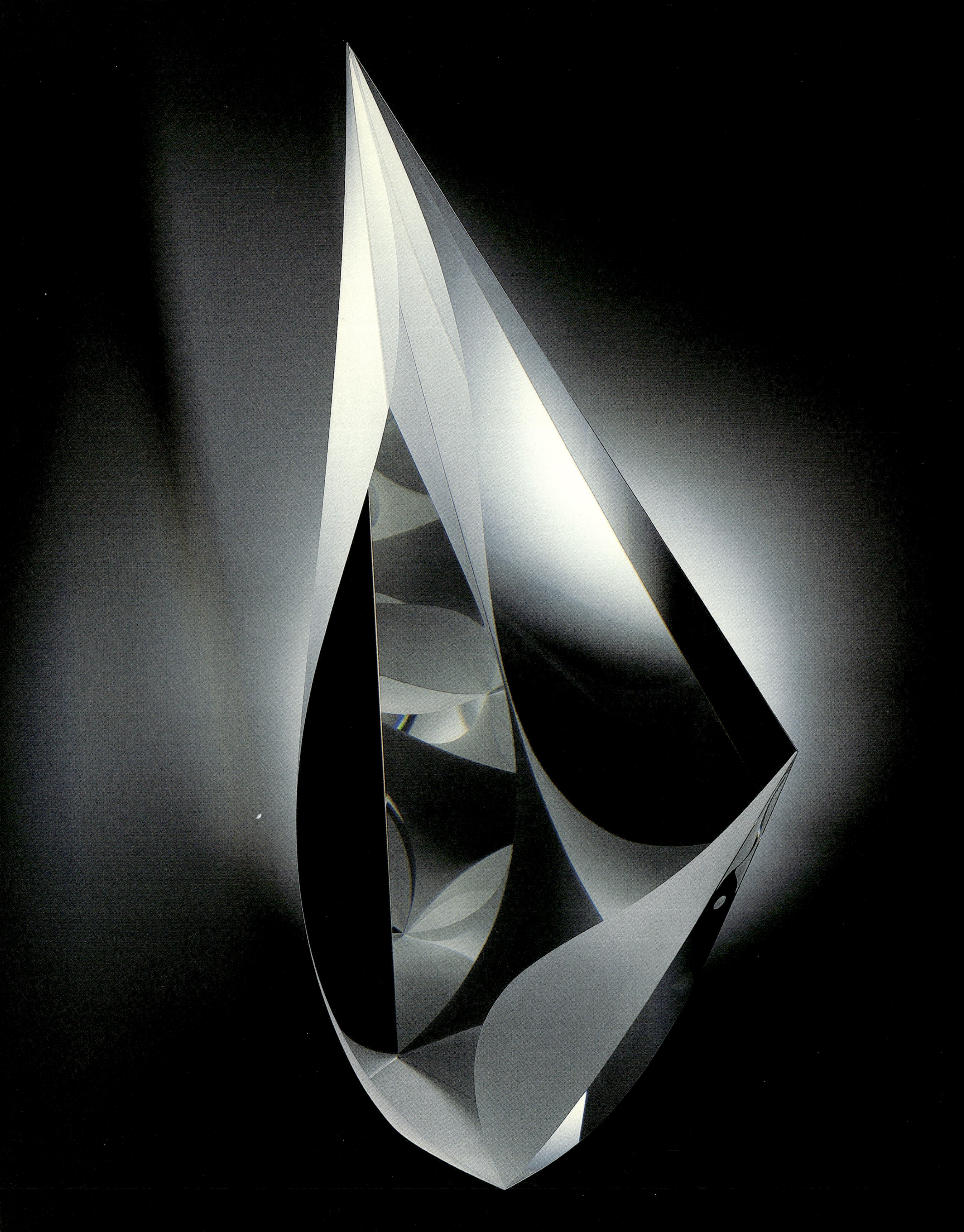

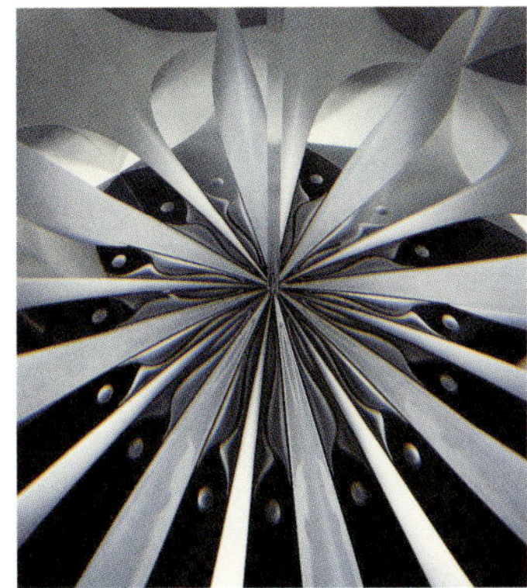

Bouquet of Light 2001

Contents

Christopher Ries with *Blue Moon* 2001

Preface and Acknowledgments

While bow fishing as a child in Little Darby Creek, Christopher Ries was captivated by the optical illusions created by light underwater. Ever since, he has been seeking to share his discoveries with anyone willing to follow him into the mystery of light as revealed through the medium of glass. Guided by this "inner necessity," a phrase borrowed from Wassily Kandinsky, Ries sought material of increasing optical purity for his sculptures. Having found a lead crystal, produced by Schott Glass Technology Inc., that transmits 99.8% of the light that strikes it, Ries has endeavored to create larger and larger pieces.

Clearly Ries takes pride in his ability to create monumental pieces from cast crystal blocks—a block, for example, that measures 43.5 x 20 x 29 inches and weighs nearly 3,000 pounds. But there is a more profound reason for his fascination with scale. With a larger work, the viewer can more readily "enter" the piece and can set up an "I-Thou" relationship with it, eliciting the desired aesthetic and spiritual experience. With scale comes weight, as may be noted in the description of the most recent pieces. But while the works are literally heavy, their essential transparency allows them to have an incredible "lightness of being," which is part of the profound meaning of the work. Finally, along with the purity of the material and the scale, Ries's inspired forms and exquisite craftsmanship are responsible for the pure visual pleasure a viewer experiences from his sculptures. The inspiration and craftsmanship are evident in both the more recent monumental sculptures and in the works in the exhibition that trace the evolution of his carved crystal sculptures, as well as in the ceramics and blown glass works with which he began his career. At a time when beauty has reentered the critical discourse about art, a reexamination of the glass sculptures of Christopher Ries seems appropriate.

The Glass Sculpture of Christopher Ries is the first major museum presentation of the artist's work since the groundbreaking exhibition, *Illusions in Glass: The Art of Christopher Ries*, mounted by Anita J. Ellis at the Cincinnati Art Museum in 1988. The catalogue, long out-of-print, remains the major source for the artist's life and work. While the Museum owns a number of Ries's early works, the source of inspiration for this exhibition was our encounter with the artist's mature monumental sculpture at the Riley Hawk Galleries several years ago. Awed by the poetry, precision, and scale of these immaculate, carved glass sculptures, we wanted to share them with our Museum audience, while also paying homage to the accomplishments of a native son and continuing our commitment to presenting the best work being done today in the medium of glass.

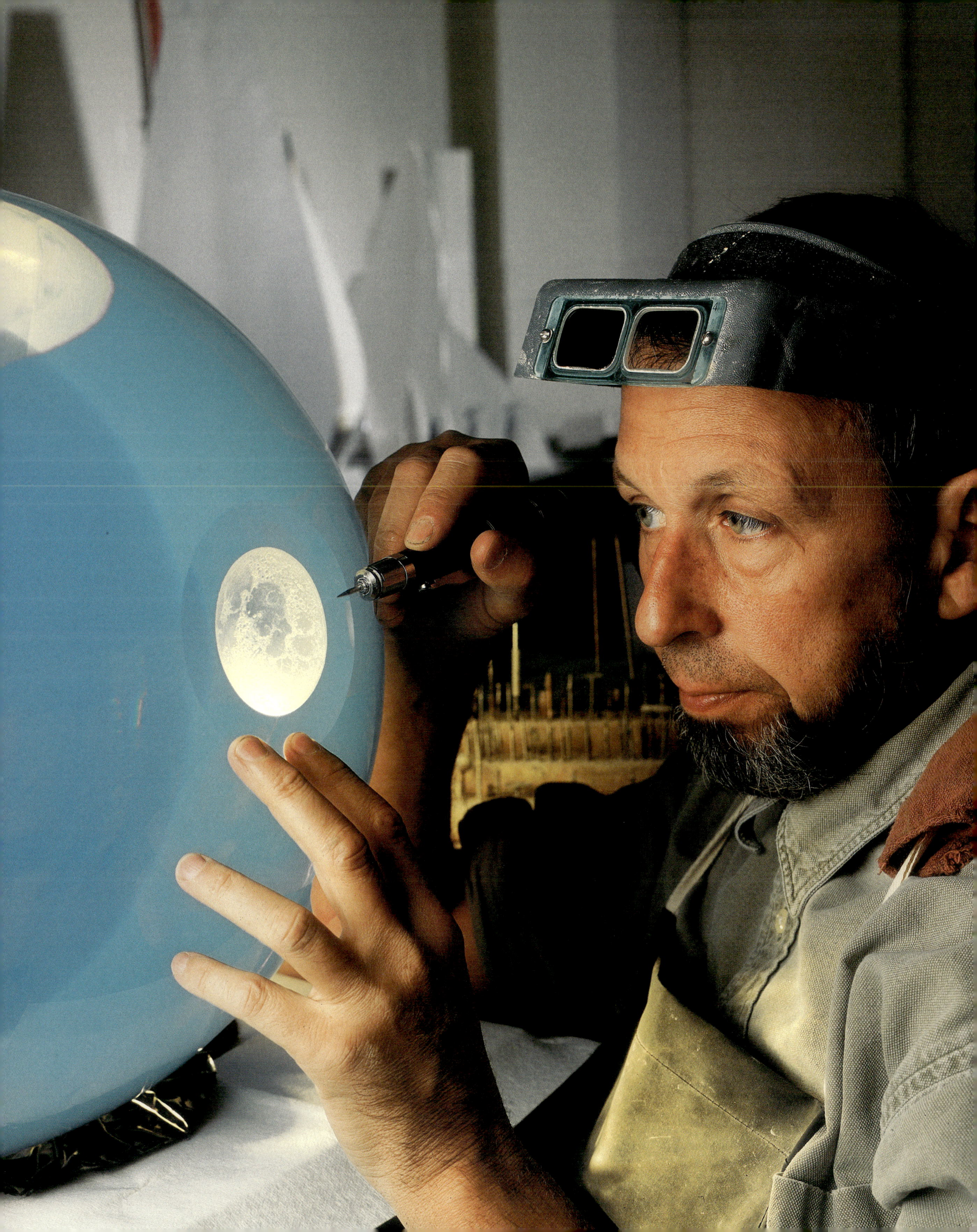

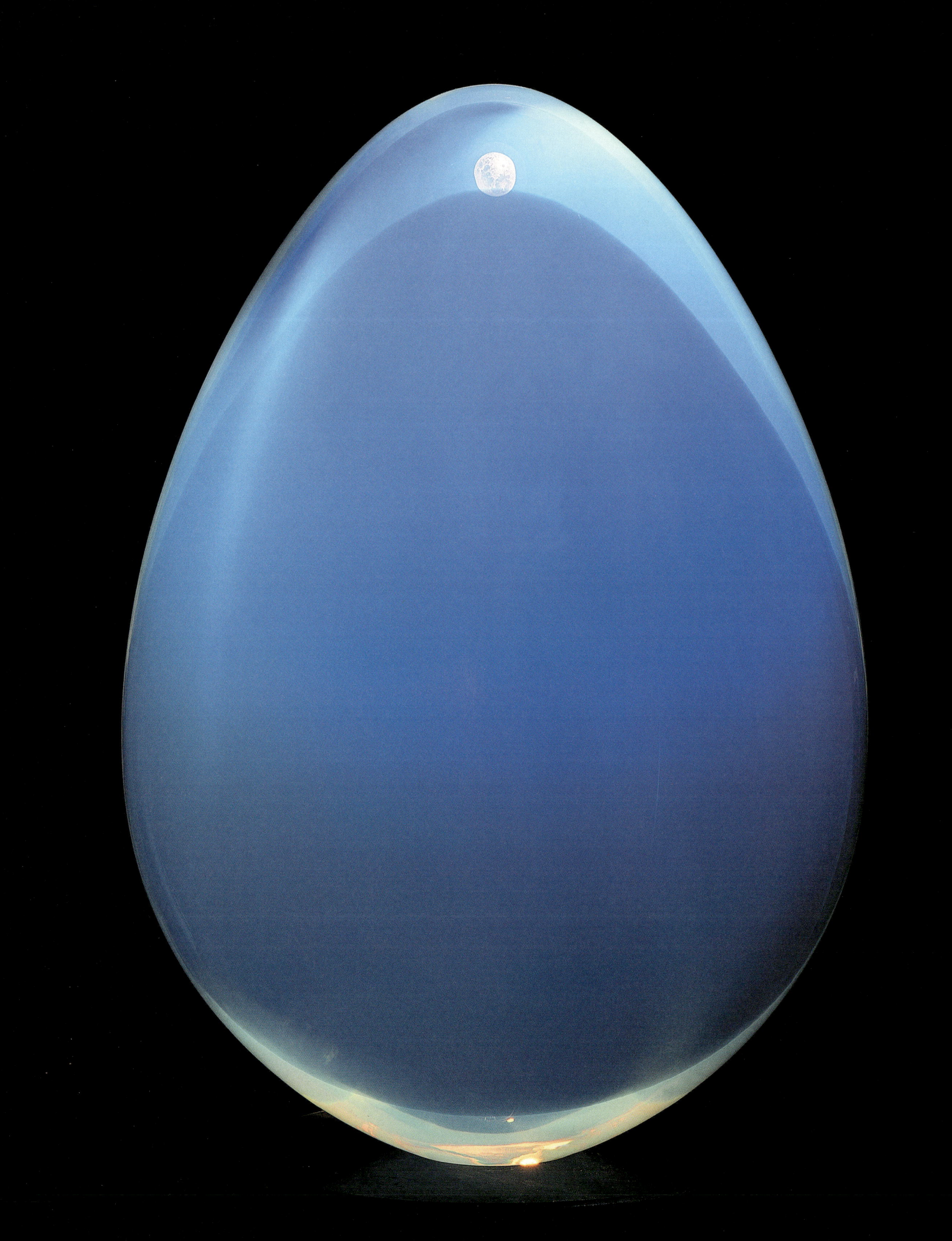

Blue Moon 2001

A project such as this involves many people. We are deeply indebted to Christopher Ries for creating a stunning group of monumental carved glass sculptures for this exhibition and for so generously lending us a group of early hand-blown glass objects from his private collection. We are also deeply grateful to the lenders of this exhibition for their willingness to part with their treasures and to share them with our Museum audience.

Our very warm thanks go to the members of the curatorial department of the Museum who were involved in the mounting of the exhibition: John Owens, head of exhibitions; Jennifer Seeds, assistant registrar; Greg Jones, exhibition designer and production manager, David Holm, exhibition design assistant; Joseph Parson, chief preparator and Darren O'Connor, preparator. Thanks, also, to Nannette Maciejunes, senior curator and director of curatorial affairs, for her support of the project.

Our gratitude also goes to Mary Elliott and Nancy Colvin of the public relations department for their help in publicizing the exhibition and to Jeff Sims, educator for adult programs, for organizing the educational component of the exhibition. Also important to the realization of the exhibition has been the support of the development department—we thank especially Lori Overmyer, director of development, and Jennifer Keefer, senior development officer.

For publication of the catalogue, we gratefully acknowledge Mrs. Richard M. Ross for the Mrs. Richard M. Ross Publications Fund of the Columbus Museum of Art. Our very warm thanks go to James Yood for his insightful essay on the life and work of Christopher Ries, "Crystal Logic"; to James Kane and Jeff Bates for translating these illusive glass sculptures into beautiful photographs; to Saul Appelbaum, curatorial assistant, for his tireless help in providing research materials and checking the many details of the biography; and to Louisa Green, the editor and head of curatorial publications. We applaud and thank Scott Gallagher and Brett Ruland for designing this truly elegant book.

On behalf of the Board of Trustees and the Museum staff, we would like to thank The Huntington National Bank for their generous lead support of the exhibition. We also thank WSYX-TV, Channel 6 and *Ohio Magazine* for promotional support; Schott Glass Technologies Inc. for their assistance on the project; and Tom Hawk and Sherrie Riley Hawk for additional support of the catalogue.

Finally, we are grateful to Colleen and Christopher Ries, their assistant Terri Walker, and David Schimmel, marketing services manager for Schott Glass Technologies, for their willingness to share their information with us and for answering endless questions.

Annegreth Nill
Curator of Twentieth-Century and Contemporary Art

Irvin M. Lippman
Executive Director

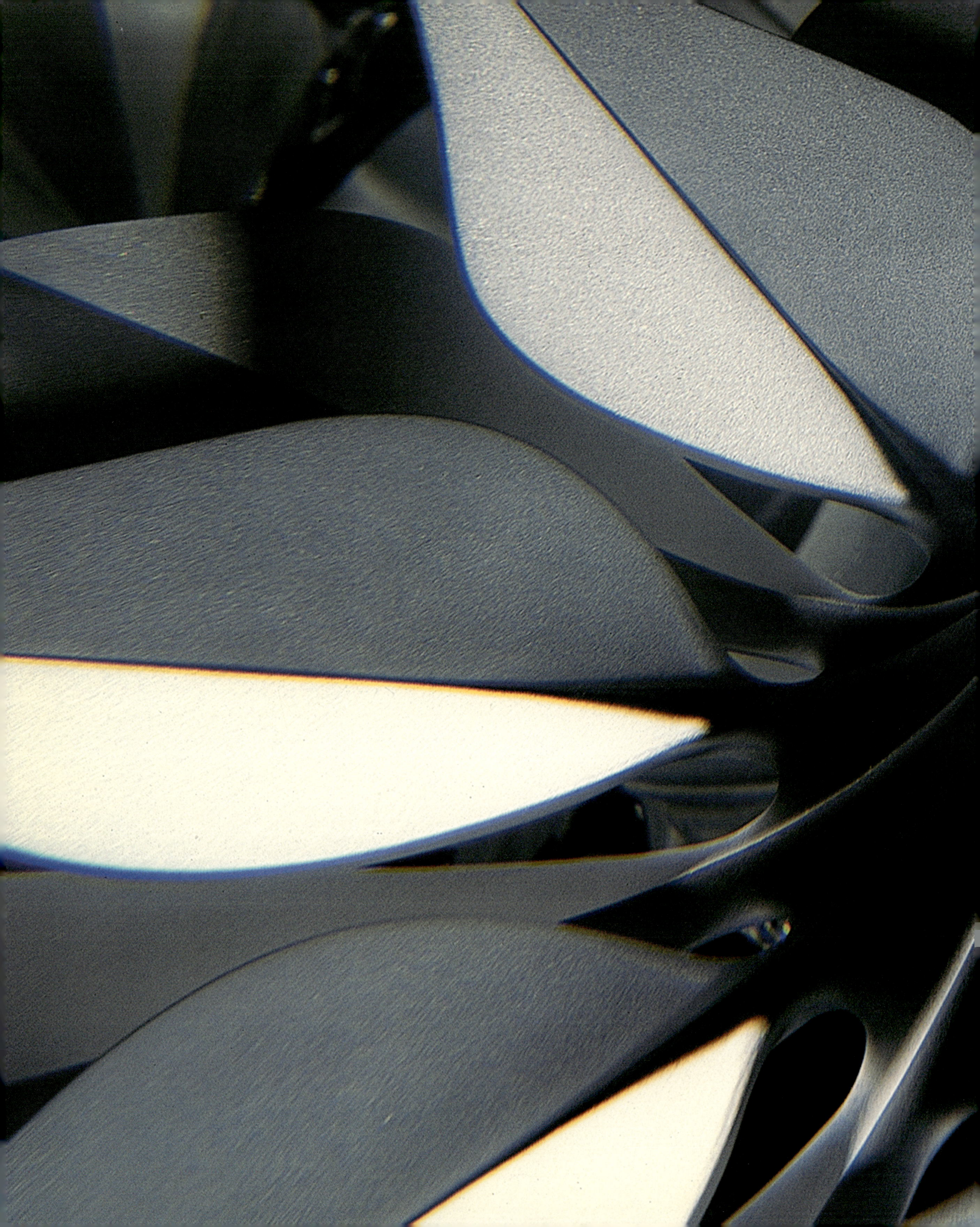

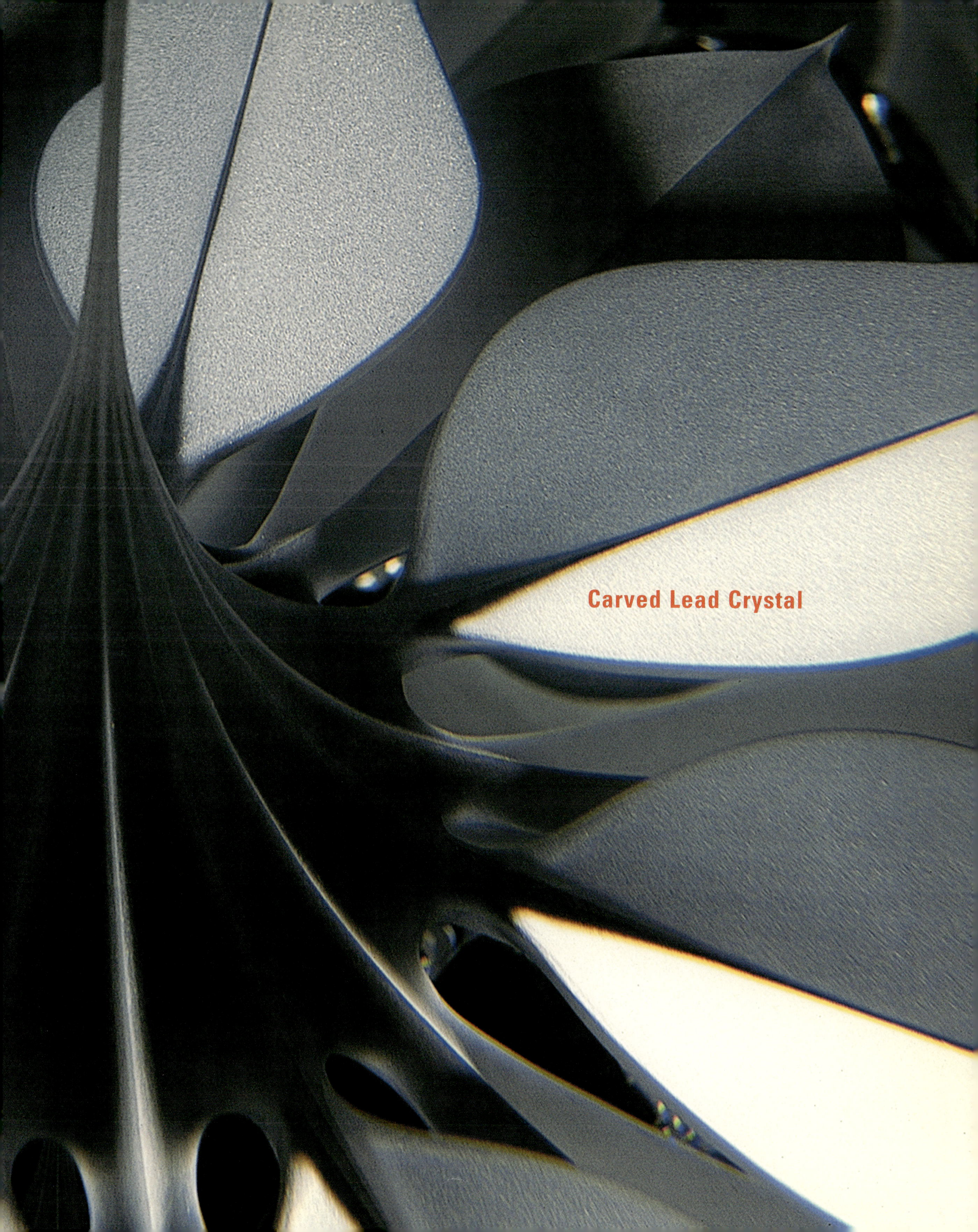

Carved Lead Crystal

Harp 2001

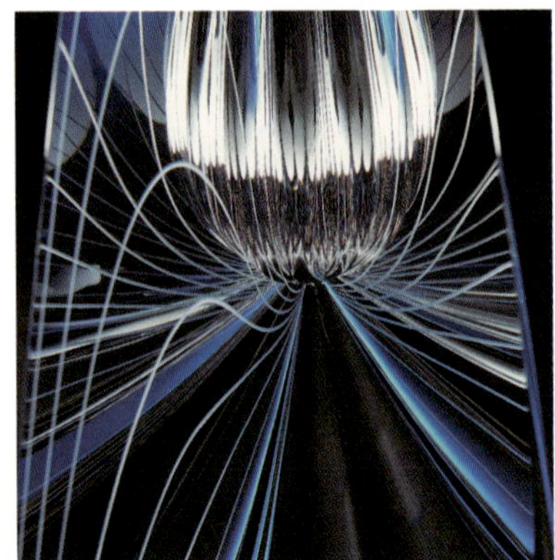

CRYSTAL LOGIC *By James Yood*

Imagine you are a beam of light. If you originated in the sun, you have already traveled some 93 million miles on your journey towards Earth. You then pass through an interruption called the atmosphere and careen and reflect around the surface of the planet. You will undoubtedly pass through one last windowpane before you enter a sculpture made of glass of such optical purity that it is 99.8% transparent.

Now you belong to Christopher Ries. Whether you've journeyed millions of miles or just a few feet from a nearby light source, he's going to bend, shape, ricochet, redirect, amplify, interrupt, mirror, and refract you. Ries will create contexts that will massage your wavelengths and make you explode in unexpected chroma. Even though you're traveling 186,000 miles per second, it will appear to you that the artist is faster, that he cunningly anticipates your every move as he sets up scenarios to maximize aspects of your photic being. It's going to seem as if at one moment he's accelerating you out of the piece like some hyper-slingshot, sending you on your merry way back into the cosmos; at the next moment he's locking you within the piece, causing you to bound and rebound in an unending chase after yourself, perhaps terminating your journey in a little bit of ground crystal. Either way, this is an art of such suggestiveness and finesse, of such ceaseless transition and surprise, that it constitutes one of the most intriguing exercises in the poetics of optics anywhere in contemporary art.

Christopher Ries does a lot of things, and among them is to create pleasingly crisp, sleek, and tapered sculptures with shapes that would be compelling and interesting no matter what their medium. But these shapes, we immediately discern, are actually stupendously crafted and scintillating platforms for cosmic bits of photo-aesthetic theater. When intersected with light, one of the most fundamental elements of the universe, Ries's shapes will spring into action. What was a form, a three-dimensional object, now revs up in crystalline proliferation, both presenting two-dimensional facets and—in its ceaseless changing as we move about it—offering an aperture into a fourth-dimensional world as well. Much sculpture is plurifacial: the artist carefully considers the presentation of the multiple profiles and shapes it will exhibit as we move about it. The sculpture of Christopher Ries, however,

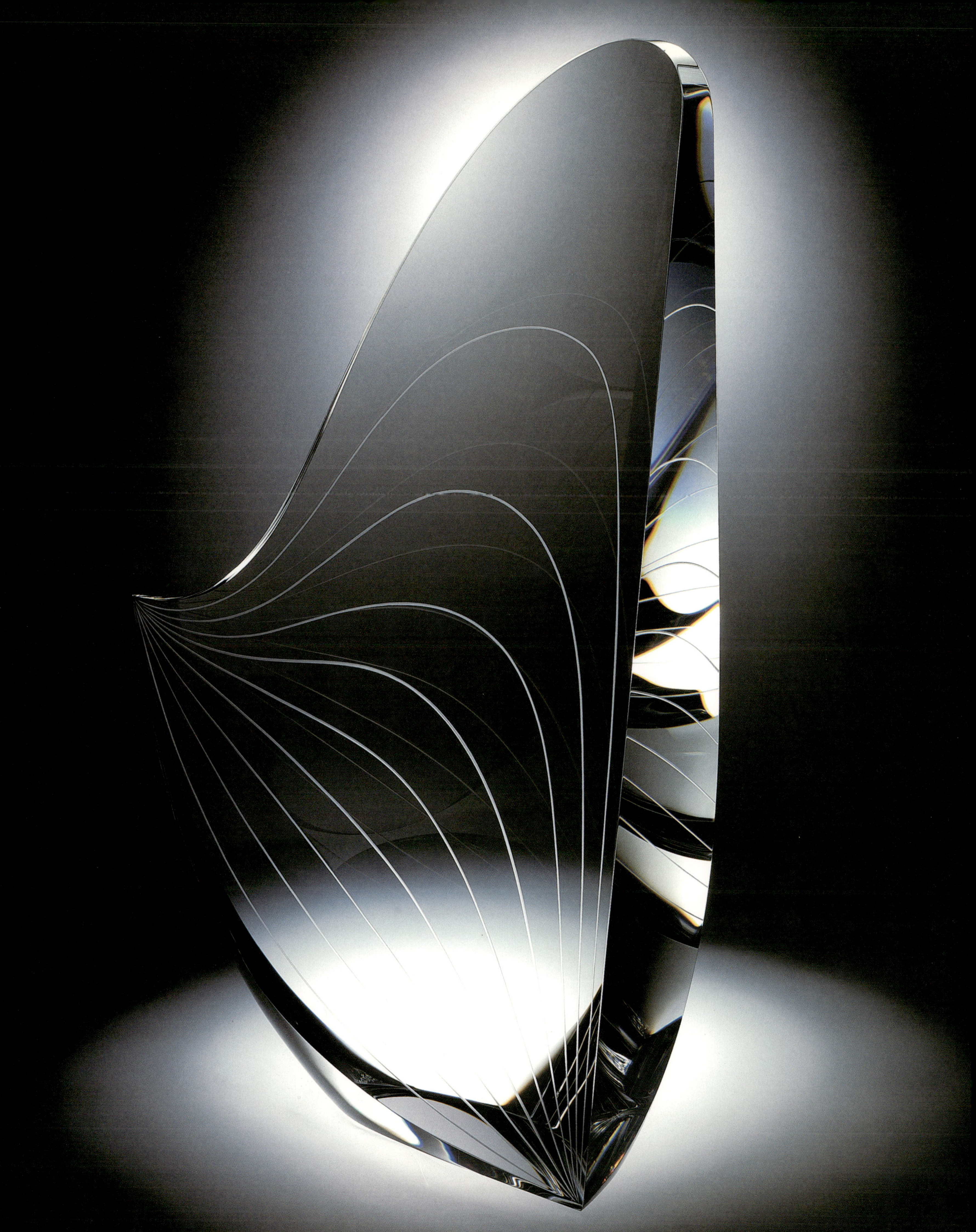

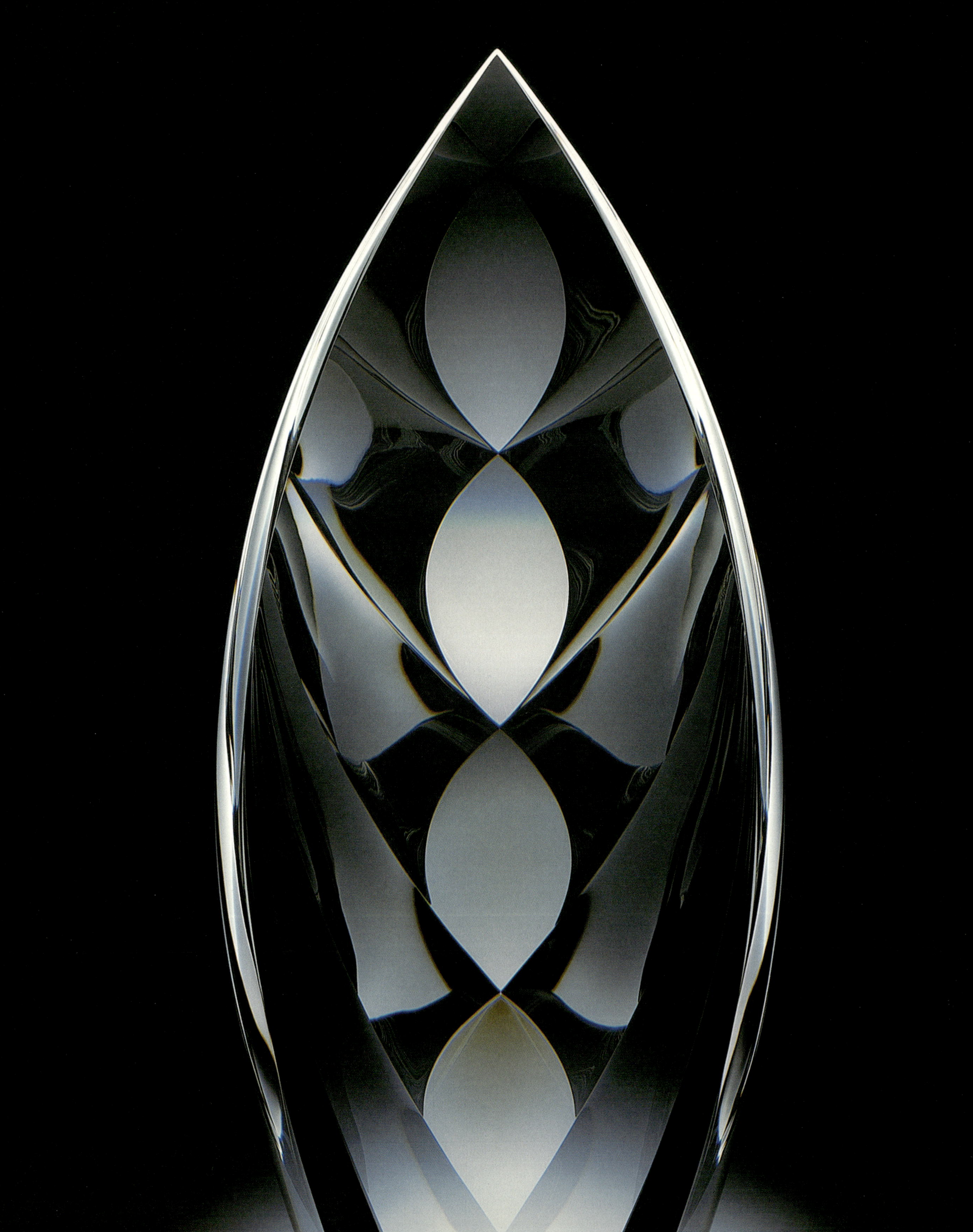

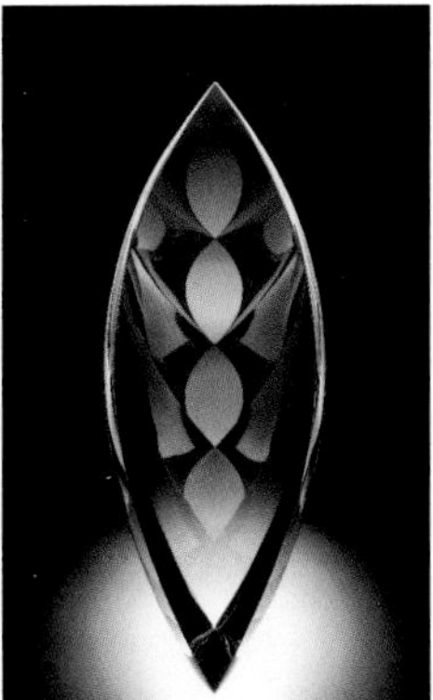

Spirit 2001

achieves an omnifacial state: it presents us with an aperture into infinity, with an exterior designed and articulated to set in motion an interior of truly endless visual incident. (It is a nicety in essays such as this to note that photography cannot ever capture the essence of sculpture, that photography's flattening effect turns the reality of three-dimensionality into fiction. This elusiveness cannot be truer than in the case of Christopher Ries. The photographs accompanying this catalog can provide no more than snippets in a chain of reception, tantalizing fragments that only hint at an experience that must happen in actual time amidst these sculptures.)

It is, of course, a particular honor for Christopher Ries to achieve this exhibition in the city that he called home for so many years. He was born and raised in the country, just a few miles west of Columbus, near the confluence of the Darby creeks. An early interest in art led Ries to nearby Ohio State University, where—and this is fairly consistent with artists who end up specializing in glass—he began by concentrating on ceramics. His interest in glass soon followed. Even while an undergraduate, he was instrumental in building a glass hot shop at OSU, and he helped teach glassblowing there before receiving his Bachelor of Fine Arts degree. He subsequently had the opportunity to study for his Master's degree with the highly respected artist Harvey Littleton, at the University of Wisconsin.

Harvey Littleton had played a central role as one of the founders of the modern studio glass movement in the United States. Beginning with his workshops at the Toledo Museum of Art in 1962, Littleton and his colleague Dominick Labino championed the possibilities for small furnace design that would liberate hot glassworking from large commercial firms and bring it to the independence of an artist's studio. Suddenly glass could become less a corporate product, less tied to the profit-driven artisanry of a large firm, and more idiosyncratic, personal, and responsive to the will of an individual artist. Ries's years with Littleton did have some aspects of an apprenticeship about them, but it was not so much a style that Harvey Littleton taught Christopher Ries as it was an attitude, the conviction that glass would be a modern material for sculpture of the highest rank. Ries became not just Littleton's student but his studio assistant, and Ries worked side by side with Littleton on many of the latter's pieces. While Littleton concentrated on the hot glasswork, among the tasks he assigned to Ries was to fabricate the bases for

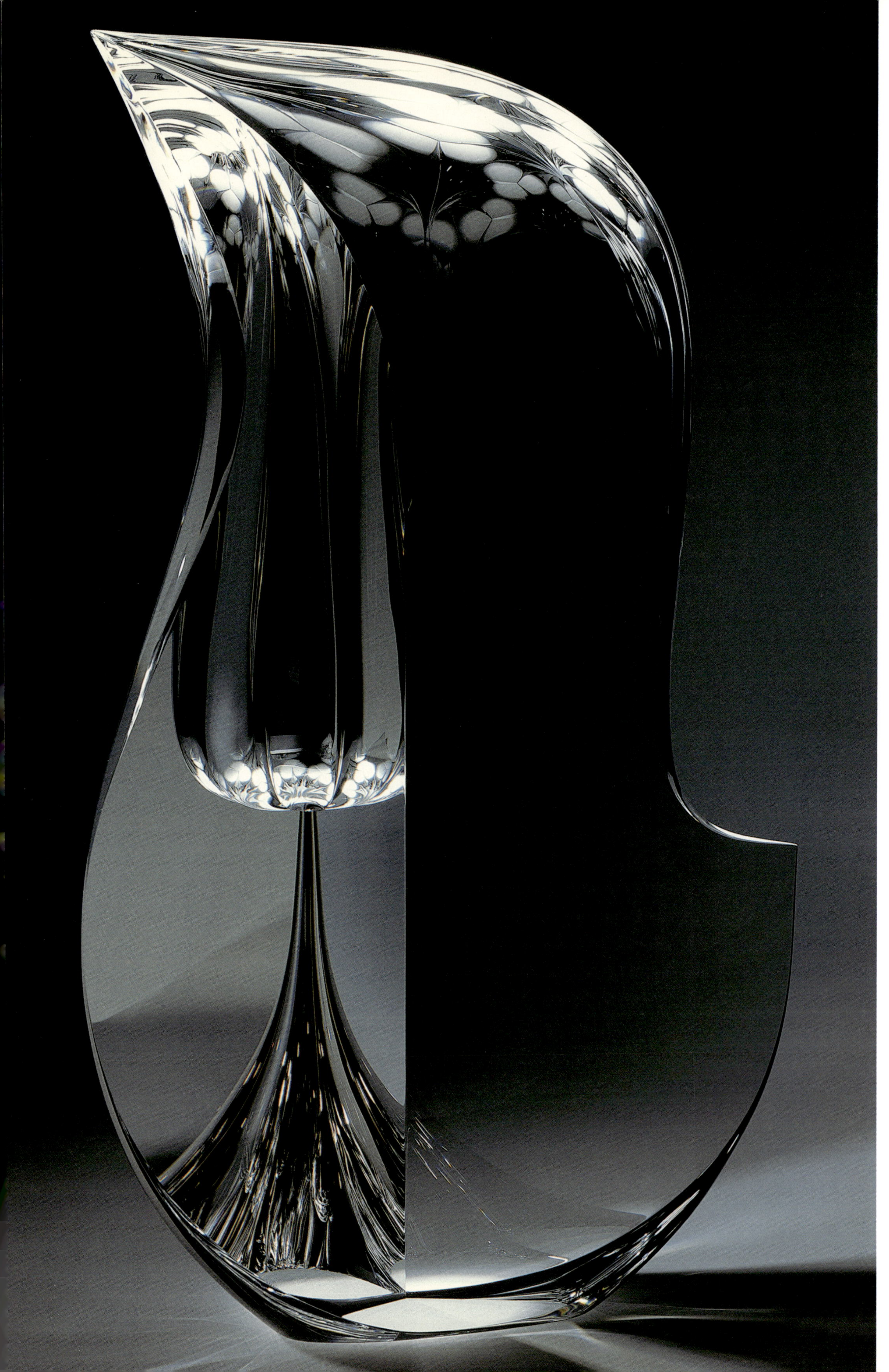

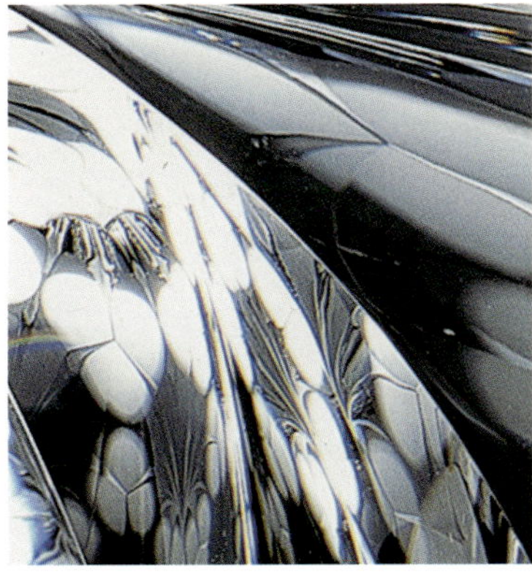

Embrace 2001

the final sculptures. Ries had grown fully conversant with all aspects of hot glasswork, but he was fascinated by this opportunity to concentrate on cold glass, to treat blocks of glass as volumetric elements that could transmit light or color. As he cut, ground, and polished these bases, Ries grew very attentive to the purity—or more often than not, the relative impurity—of the glass he was using. He noticed how tiny imperfections imbedded in the block would become amplified and distorted, and he realized how soupy and muddy most of the glass that we assume to be transparent actually is. (Standard window glass, for example, only successfully transmits about 70 percent of the light that enters it; we tend not to notice this effect because of the thinness of most windowpanes.)

While attending the University of Wisconsin, Ries helped to build and maintain a studio in nearby Mineral Point, Wisconsin, and he spent two summers working both hot and cold glass there, before moving back to Columbus. He continued his researches into the technology of glass fabrication, its chemistry, and its optical and physical properties, educating himself about the visual potentials of crystal. Seeking a purer form of glass for his investigations, Ries began communicating with commercial enterprises that manufactured glass for scientific and technological purposes. One such firm, Schott Glass Technologies Inc., in Duryea, Pennsylvania (near Scranton/Wilkes-Barre), would change his life.

Schott is an international firm with sales to industry and government currently exceeding $2 billion. As their Web site puts it, Schott specializes in "a commitment to the enhancement of glass and glass ceramics to meet the needs of advancing technology." Schott glass was used in the lenses of the cameras the astronauts took to the moon, and Schott's current work in fused silica and laser glass may hold a key to finding cleaner and cheaper sources of energy. Much of Schott's research would remain beyond Ries's ken, but he responded avidly to the search for absolute clarity in the glass that Schott produced, seeing in it a raw material from which he could cajole optical effects of the most exciting sort.

Schott, of course, had little experience in meeting the needs of an individual creative artist. When Ries first contacted the firm in the late 1970s, the firm was cooperative enough to give and later sell him chunks of what was by far the purest glass he had ever seen. Ries's relationship with Schott has now lasted some twenty years. He began visiting the firm regularly in 1982, commuting from his home in Columbus, and he became artist-in-residence to Schott Glass Technologies in 1986, a position he continues to hold today. In 1992 he and his family moved to Pennsylvania. Ries is not an employee of Schott, but rather an ongoing guest, an autonomous agent with a studio on the premises of the firm. Ries developed a financial relationship with Schott that provides him with glass and access to their highly sophisticated tools and facilities in return for a certain percentage of the income generated by the sale of his art. This arrangement allows him to work on a scale he could never realize otherwise and to create pieces that can weigh several hundred pounds.

The relationship between Schott and Ries represents one of the most interesting, and symbiotic corporate/artistic intersections in the world today; art and commerce work here side by side, the artist receiving access to materials and machinery he could not afford on his own, the firm finding prestige in a cultural application of their technology they never anticipated. Even the financial relationship seems a model of its type, as the artist is not dependent on corporate largesse but is a professional partner in production and display.

Philosophically, this consensual return to the factory is an intriguing anomaly in the development of the modern studio glass movement. While Littleton's researches into small studio furnaces have provided a tremendous impetus to independent and isolated studio practice, the exodus from the glass factory has meant leaving a certain amount of technological expertise behind. What Christopher Ries (trained in that studio milieu) enjoys at Schott is a bit of the best of both worlds. Schott is certainly not a glassworks that creates domestic ware for sale; it is a laboratory at the cutting edge of crystal technology. There Ries speaks and interacts every day not with artists but with scientists and professionals who are seeking new horizons for glass, subjecting it to new applications in pursuit of new possibilities. The ethos Ries encounters there—the corporate penchant for logic, exactitude, crispness, and precision—becomes part of the ethos of his own work, dovetailing perfectly with his own quest for a poetics of purity.

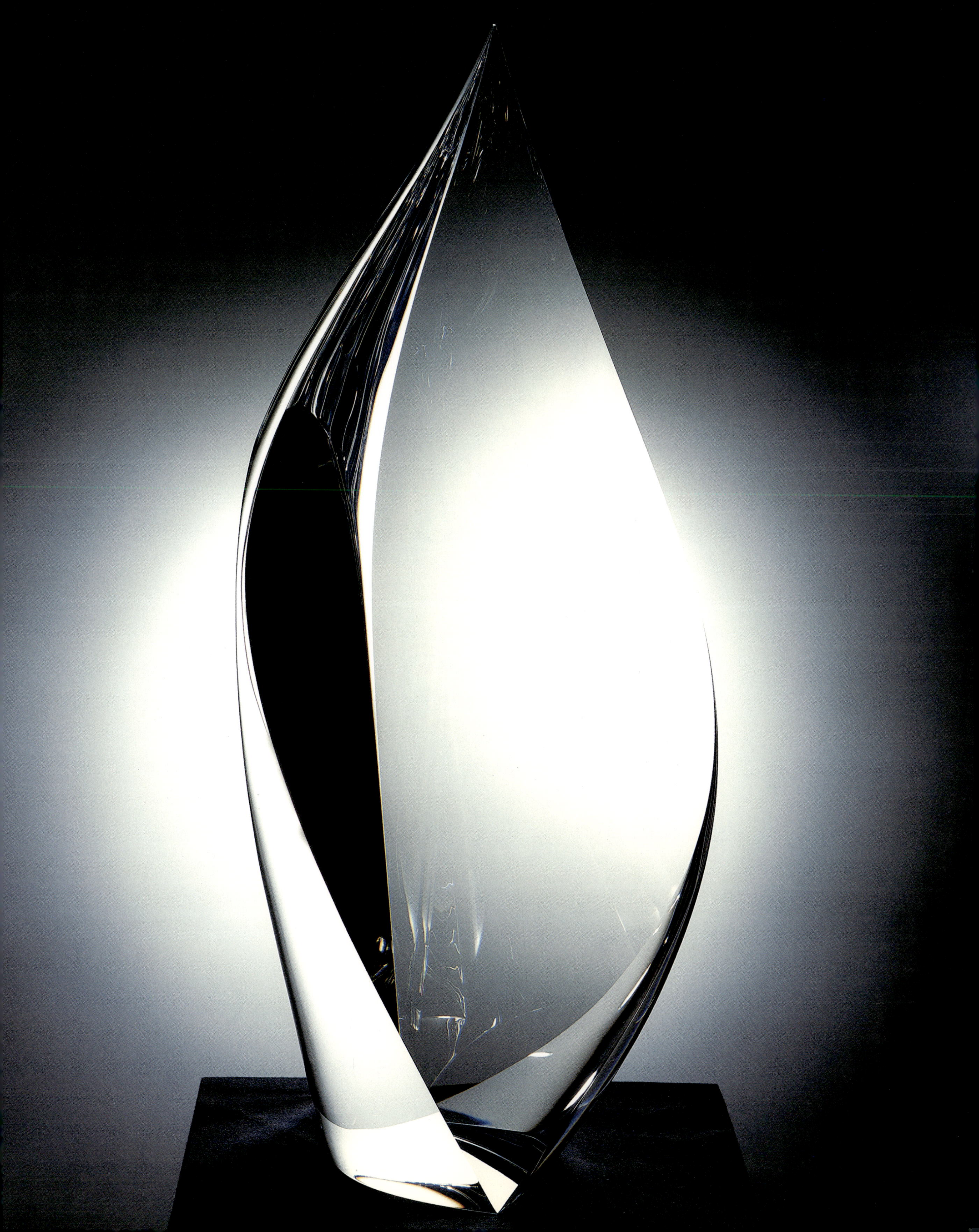

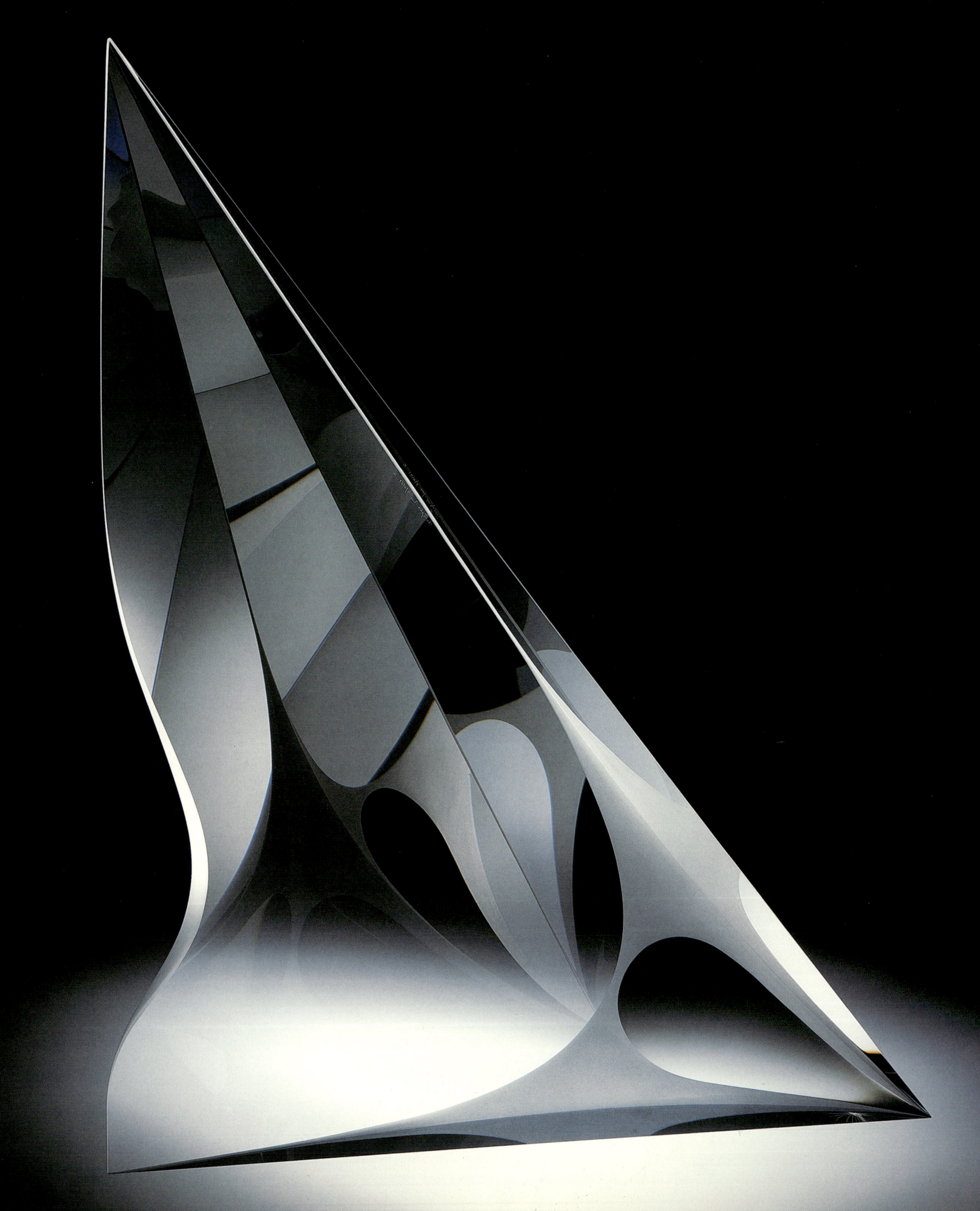

A work by Christopher Ries, especially the large-scale pieces on display in this exhibition, begins with the creation of a block of glass that exhibits state-of-the-art/industry homogeneity and clarity. The block will never solarize, never get dingy—the purity of the material allows it to transmit 99.8% of the light. The block can often weigh more than 3,000 pounds, and it can take several months in an annealing chamber to cool from its molten state to room temperature, until it is stable. Then Ries subjects that block to an incredible and complex sequence of sawing, grinding, cutting, carving, sanding, and polishing, very often in several repeated stages and levels. This highly skilled assault on the block can take him and his assistants a year or more to complete. The slightest error—a scratch, a chip, a flaw discovered within the glass, an improperly ground edge—renders the piece useless, and the artist does have to contend with a certain percentage of false starts. This part of the process is all coldworking; once the glass is cast as a block, heat plays no subsequent role in the creation of these sculptures.

But it is not technology, however interesting and complex, that makes Christopher Ries a sculptor of note—it is what he does with and through that technology. He is a conjurer, a releaser, and a seeker endlessly fascinated and moved by the optical mystery of light. He wants to caress it, turn it this way and that, surprise it, try to bend it to his will, and set it in an engagement with itself that will allow us to apprehend the essence of its metamorphic being. Glass and light—that's all Christopher Ries uses. He tends to avoid color, laminate, and other materials, reducing his components to their essential elements and then showing how endless is their interplay. Skill by skill, effect by effect, he has uncovered how a sliver here, a triangulation there, a beveled edge at that point, a swelling of material over here, a long surface plane on this side, an abrupt incision at that base, a bit of engraving at that spot, now concave, now convex, will provide the intensified prismatic aperture that allows his highly directed magic to happen. Ries is a chessmaster who through long and diligent practice has trained himself to think several moves ahead; his mind senses what light might do next and how glass can be sculpted to permit or frustrate its procedures—how form can be tied to function. But he knows simultaneously that light can be infinite in its possibilities, that every angle of incidence, secondary light source, change of environment, time of day, even a nearby wall and the viewer's height and shadow, can re-spin the agenda into something new, something never seen before. Each piece by Ries exists solely for the immediate viewer, who sees something unique, different from what the next person will experience, as he or she circles about the sculpture while it performs its intimate dance for that viewer alone. The contour of the piece itself never changes, while the light intersecting it will change, as will the position of the viewer's eyes and mind, as he or she circumnavigates this always transmutative object.

Falling Petals 2001

A payoff for all this creative effort is sometimes a sudden glimpse of a skillfully articulated shape, a crystalline rendition of a vase, flower, bird, angel, or body, an eerie and transitory image that will disappear as soon as the viewer moves an inch or two away. There is, of course, no vase or flower or bird, but a bit of ground or contoured glass that immediately and momentarily calls up the image—fully coalesced. The image is evanescent and fragile, this little ode to form, a kind of spirit called out of geometry, a pulsation frozen within the solidity of glass. You look in vain across the surface of the piece to find that shape somehow etched or secreted, probably realizing that it will never be there, that what you find in that one moment of cohesion is itself a compilation of fragments, constructed out of reflections and refractions that are dazzlingly mirrored about.

Often, too, Ries gives us pure abstraction, a piling-up of angles, lines, curves, and arcs that makes the viewer feel he or she is caught in a Lyonel Feininger painting with no way out. Or we could think of these more abstract pieces in relation to gem working, to the jeweler's search for a dizzying cacophony of faceting. But while a jeweler is usually satisfied with the proliferation of facets in pursuit of surfeit, that way is never Ries's. His work is not about how many bits of incident he can create in the pieces, but which of those bits are right and judicious enough to further his ideas. At times he does want to multiply light in an intense fit of velocity. More often, however, he will choose to vary its rhythms to display the range of possibilities that occur when light intersects with carefully prepared volumes of glass.

If no light falls upon a sculpture by Christopher Ries, does it achieve the status of art? This question is more than one of those conundrums such as the one about the tree-falling-in-the-forest. Art always requires light to render it visible. But the sculptures of Christopher Ries are not merely illuminated by light, they are set into kinetic motion by it, and they begin to manifest themselves. Illumination can be both a thing and a state of being. In both cases, light—exterior and interior—is the metaphoric vehicle we use to describe illumination's journey. The sculptures of Christopher Ries allow light to reveal its architecture, logic, and steadfastness, while preserving its mystery and spirit. He gives us, in a way, a charged intersection of the psychology of light and of the person who receives it, providing a context for the sequential contemplation of aspects of the mechanics of life and light, two of the grandest creations in the universe.

James Yood teaches contemporary art theory and criticism at Northwestern University. He writes regularly for *Artforum* and *GLASS* magazines.

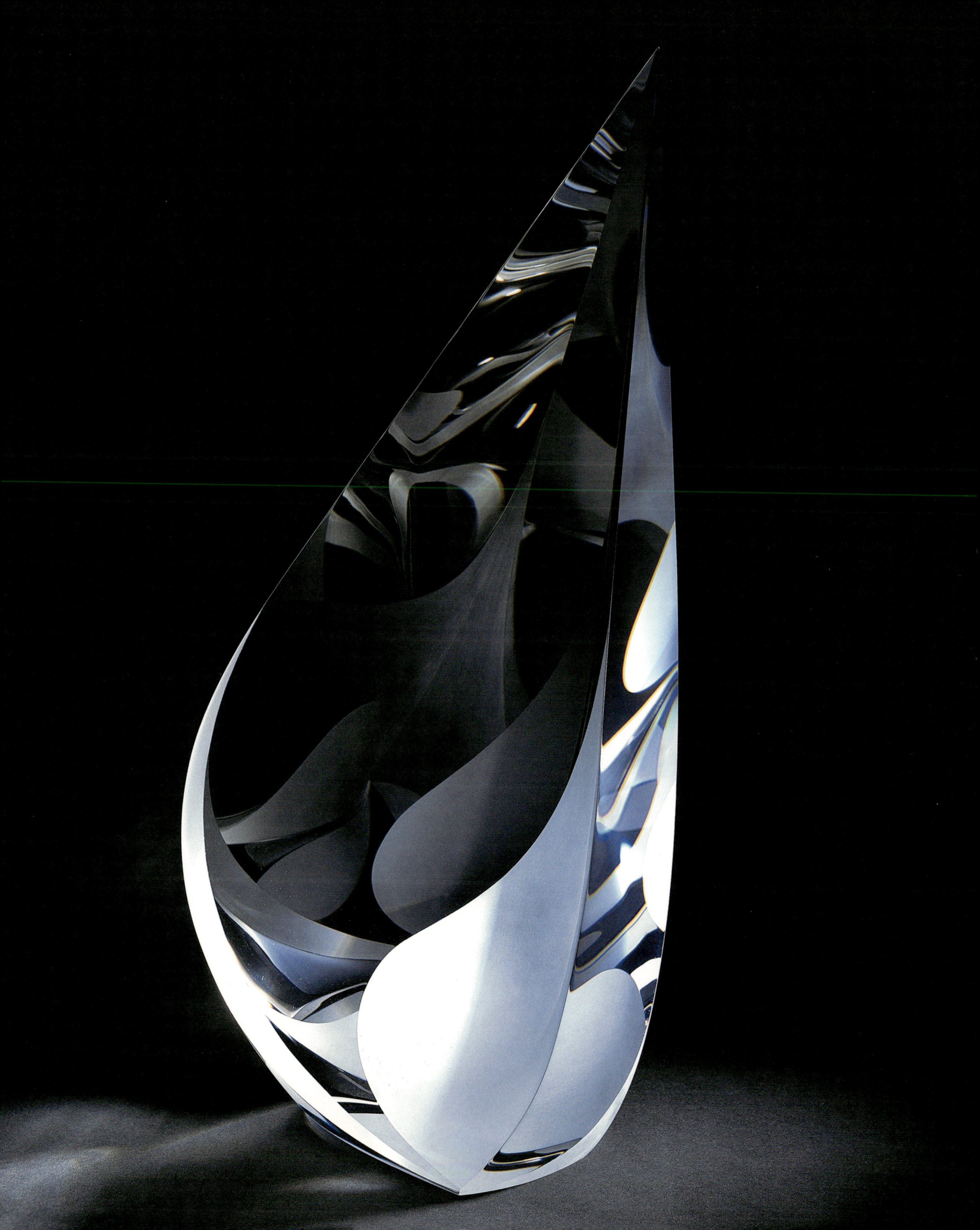

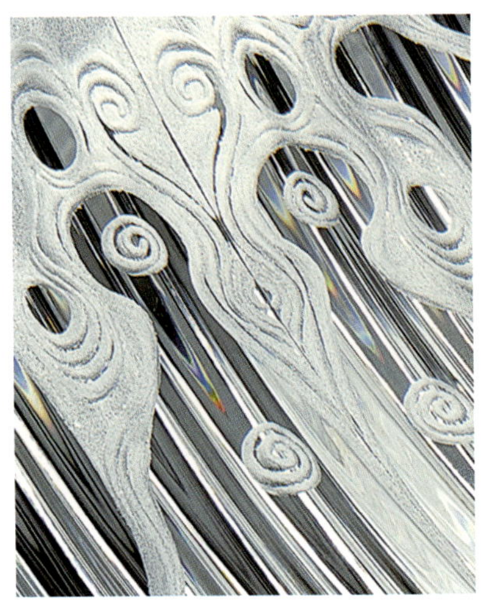

Mezzo Luna 2000

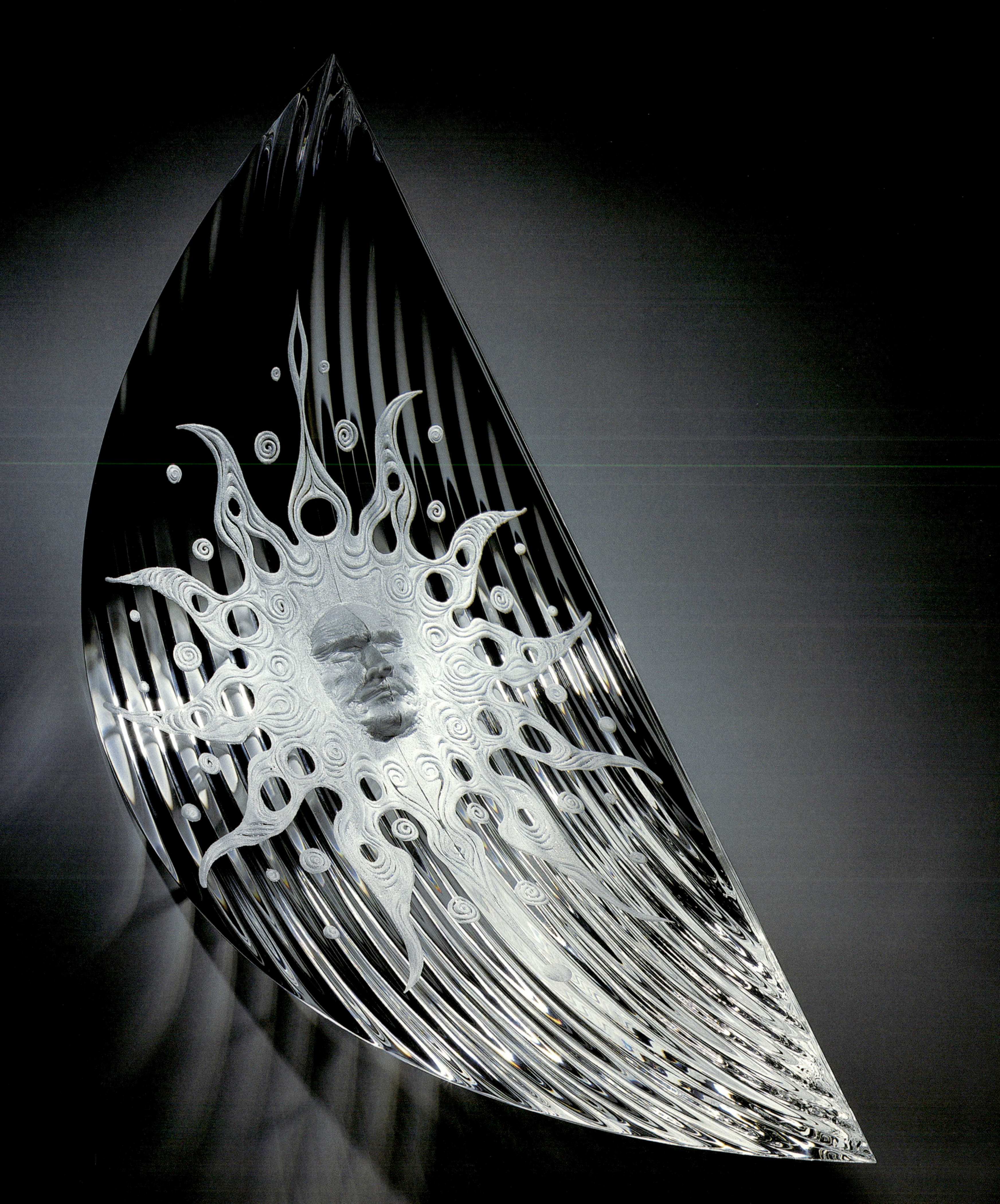

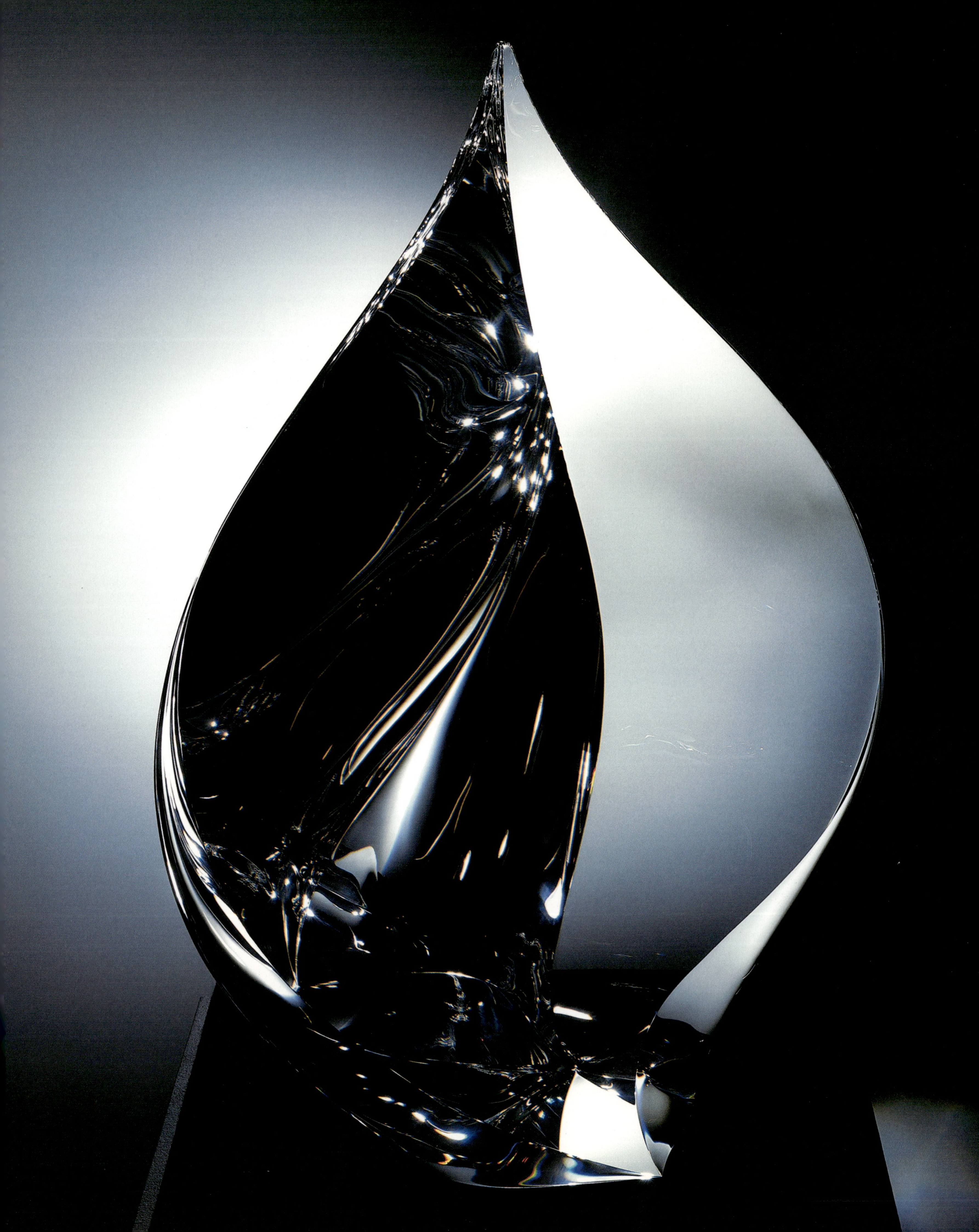

Afterglow 1999

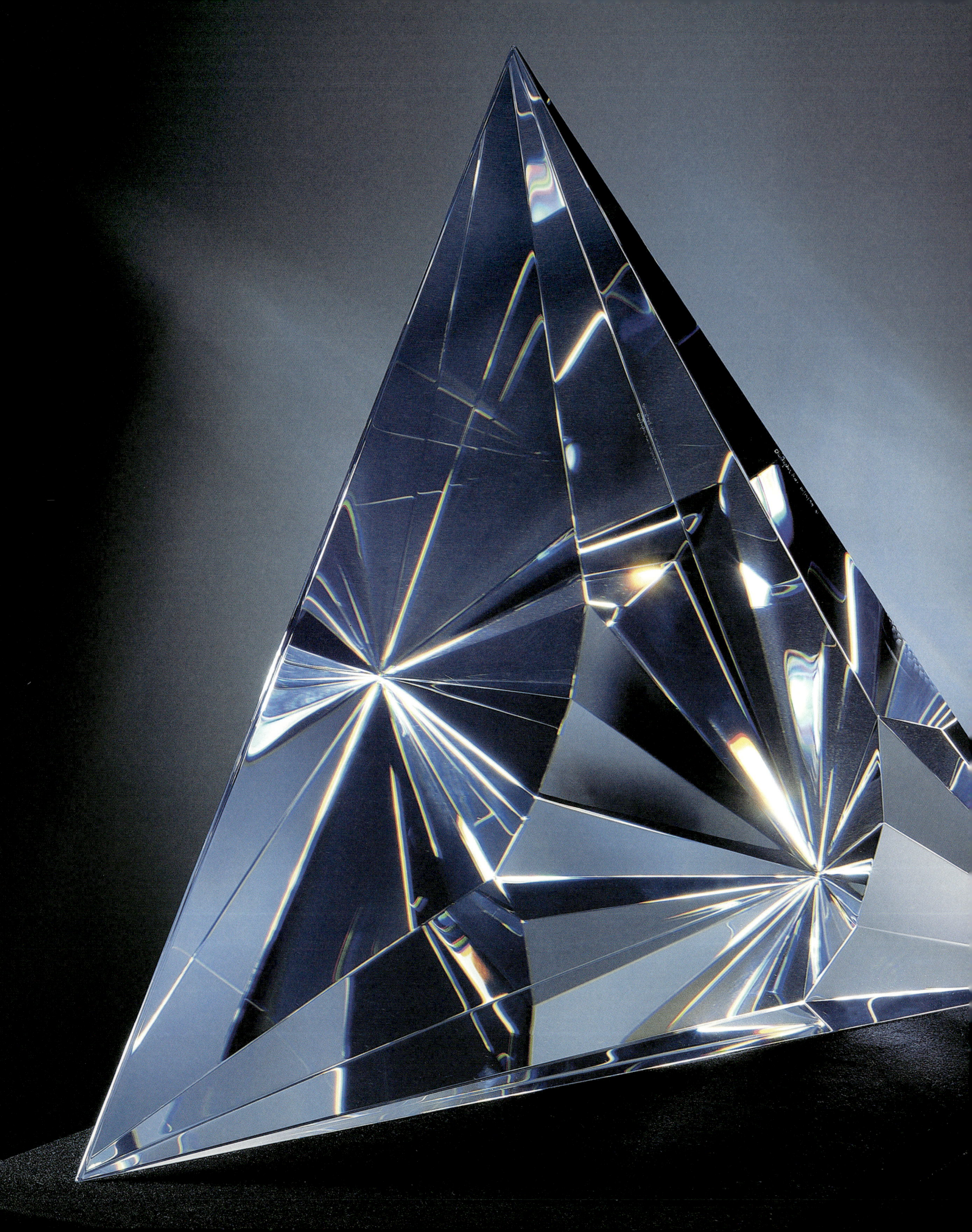

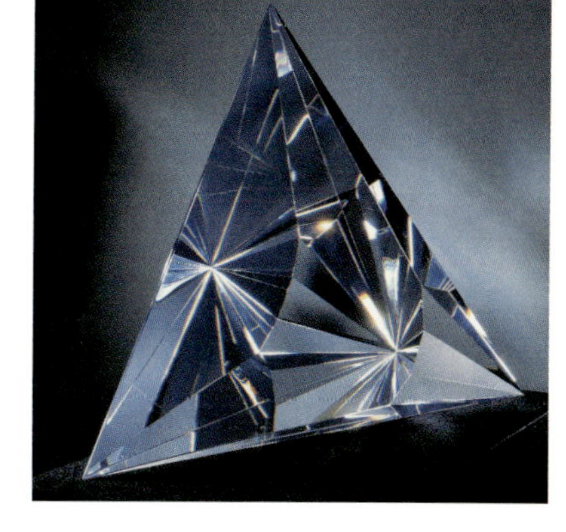

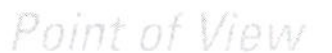

Point of View 1999

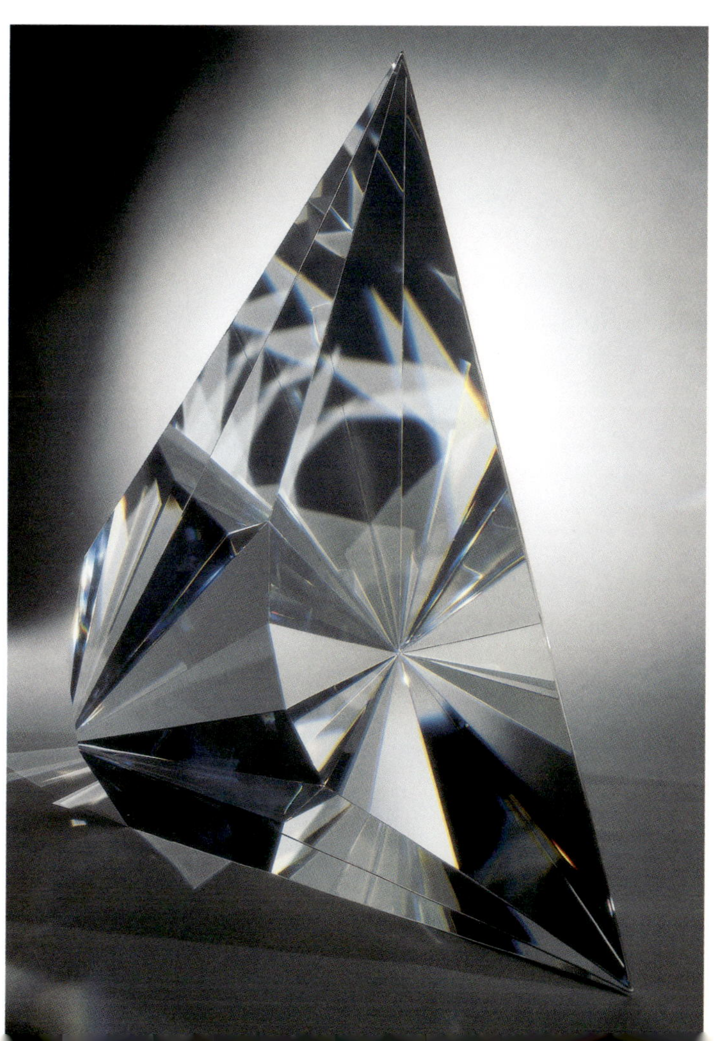

Pacific Flora 1999

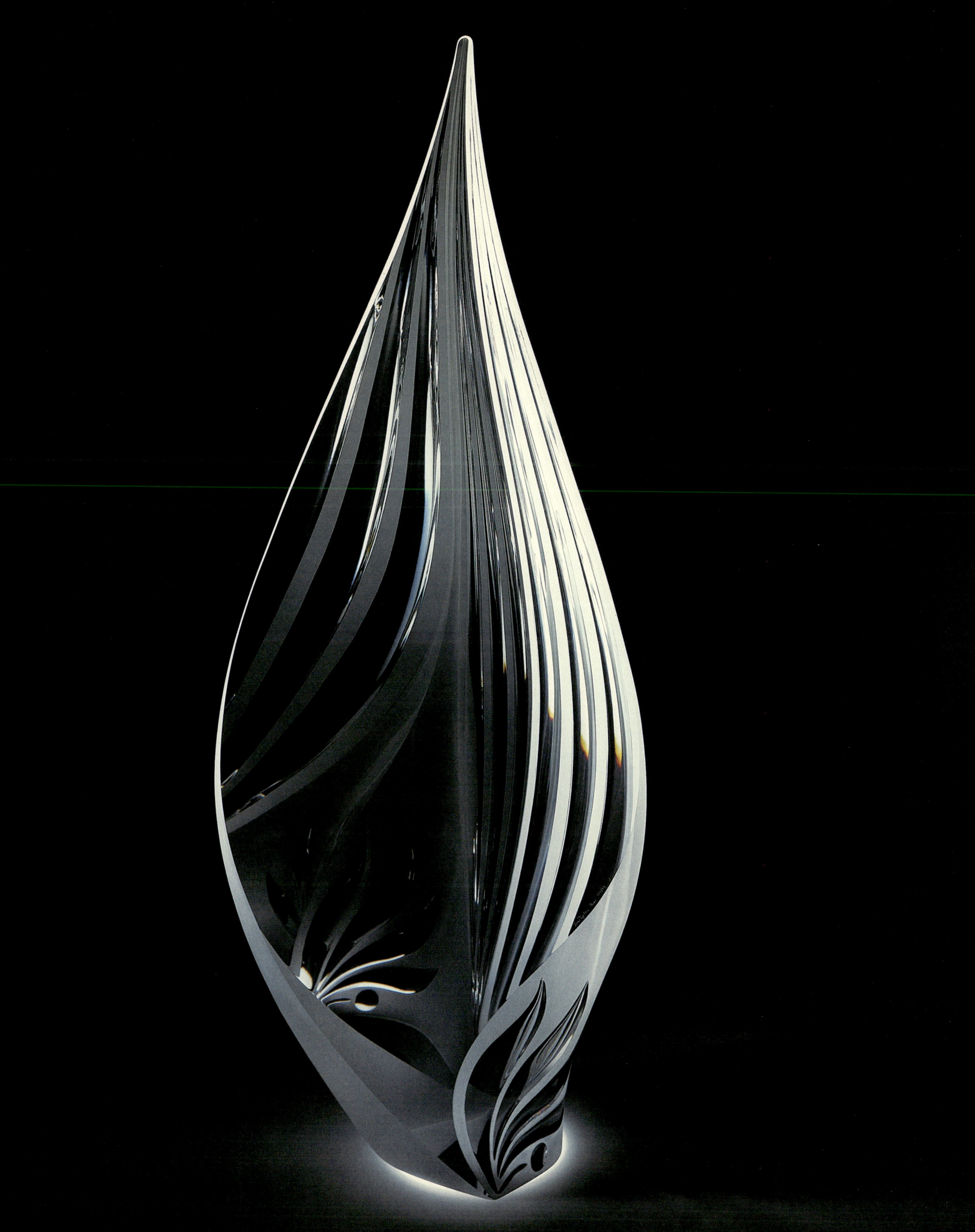

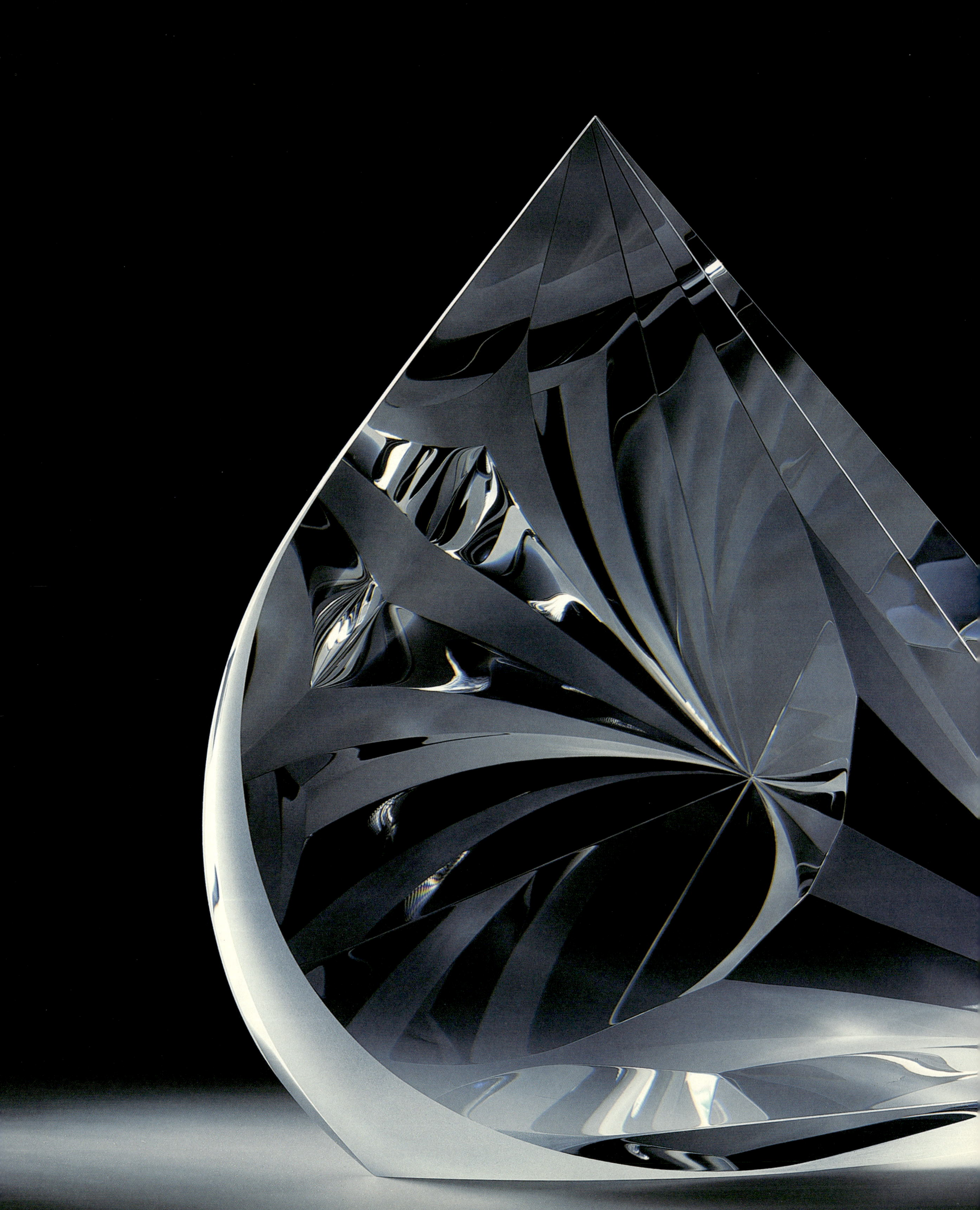

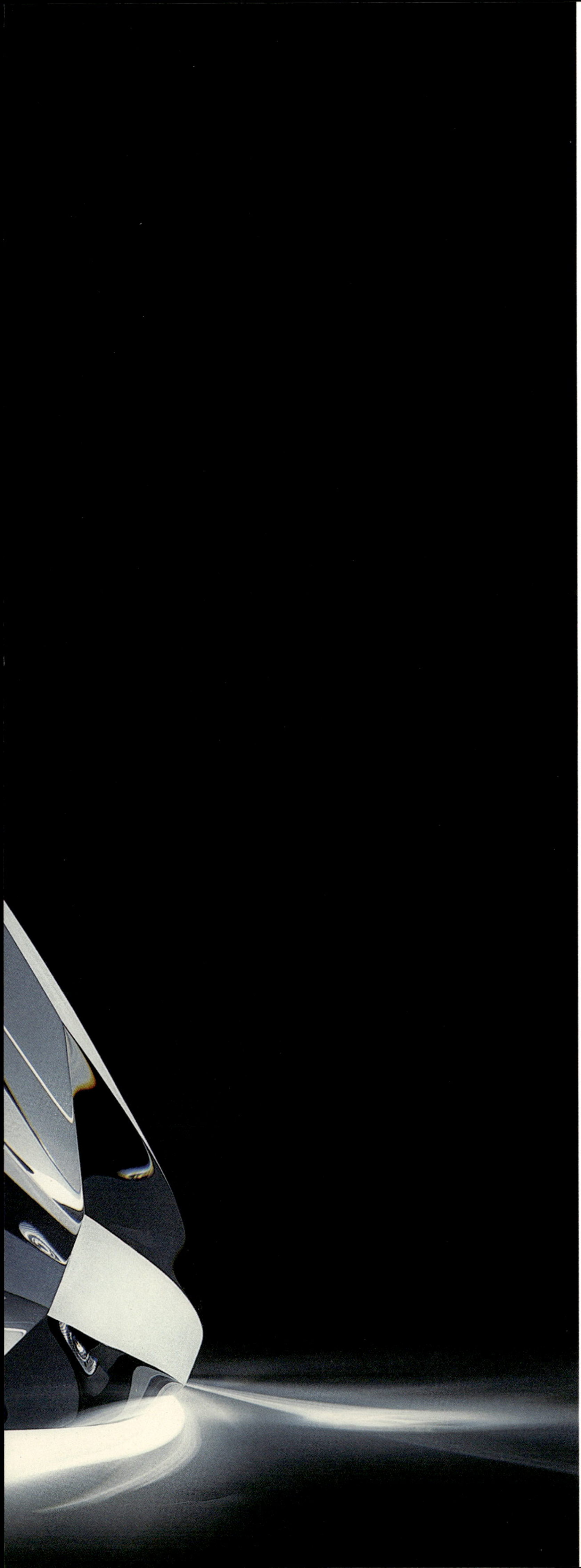

Celebration 1999

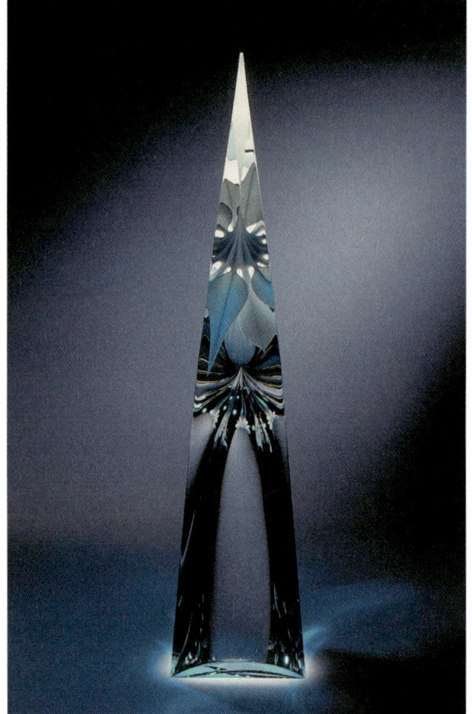

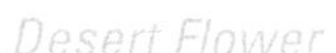
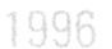
Desert Flower 1996

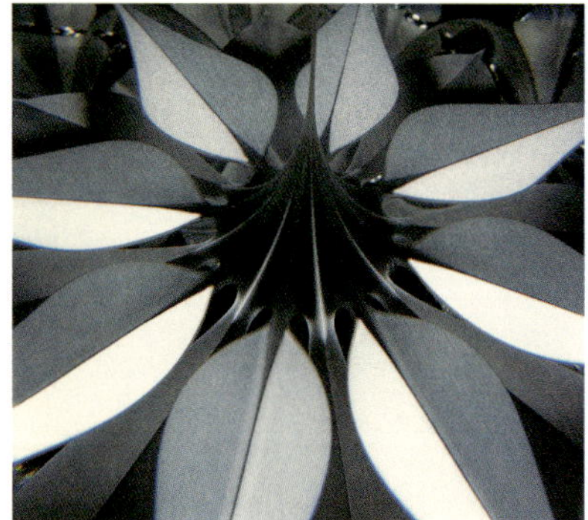

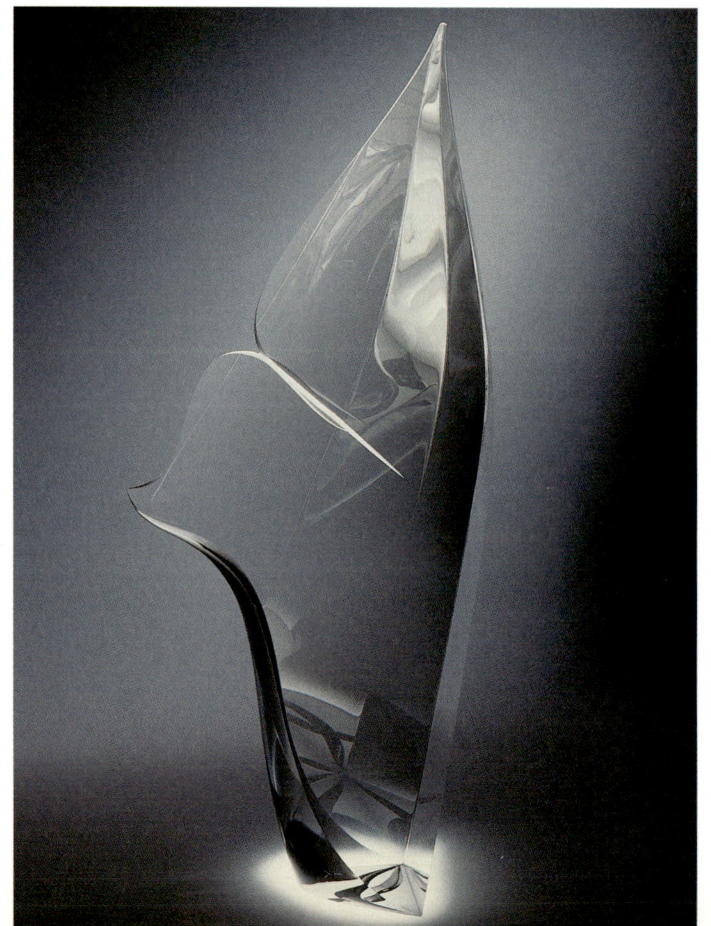

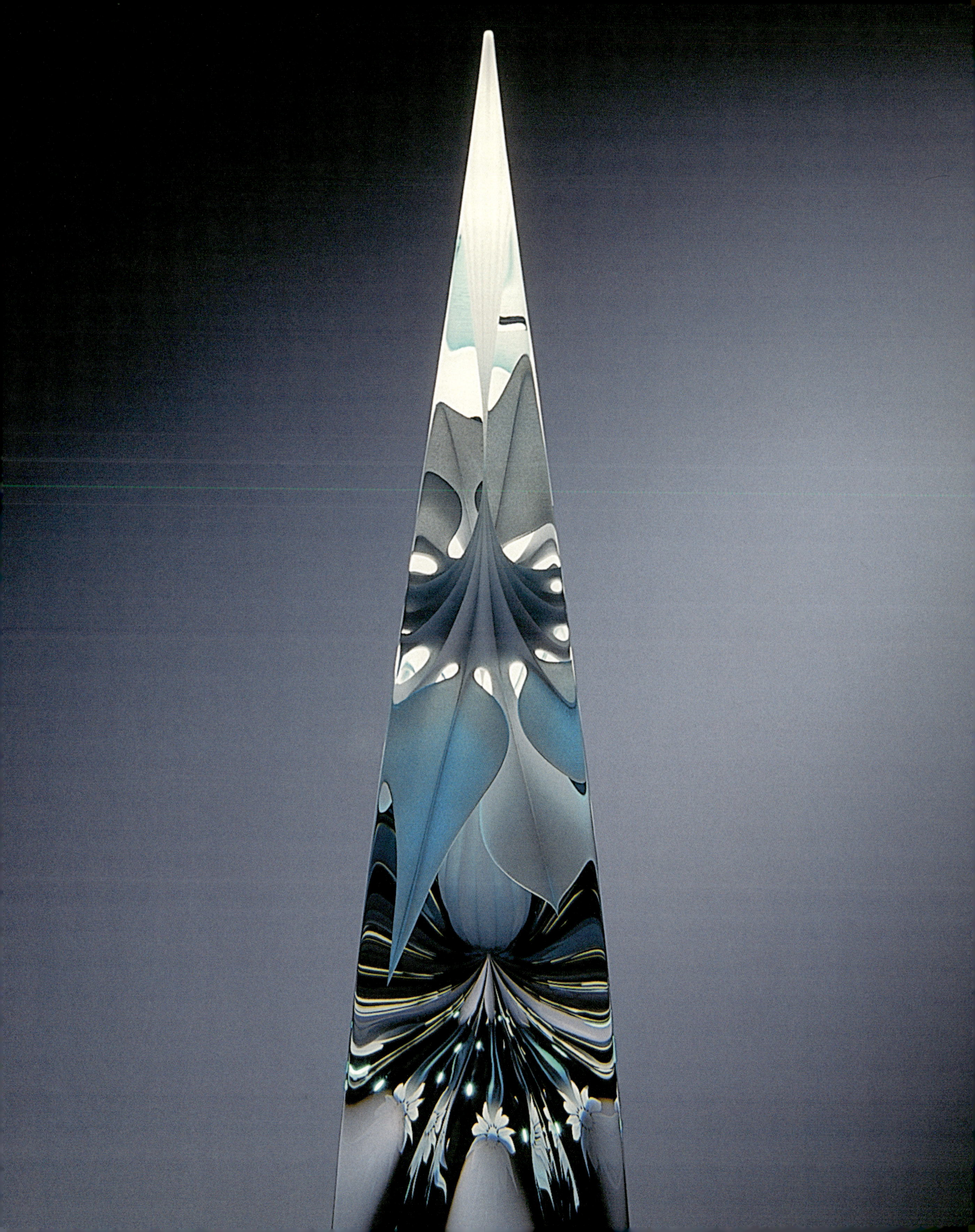

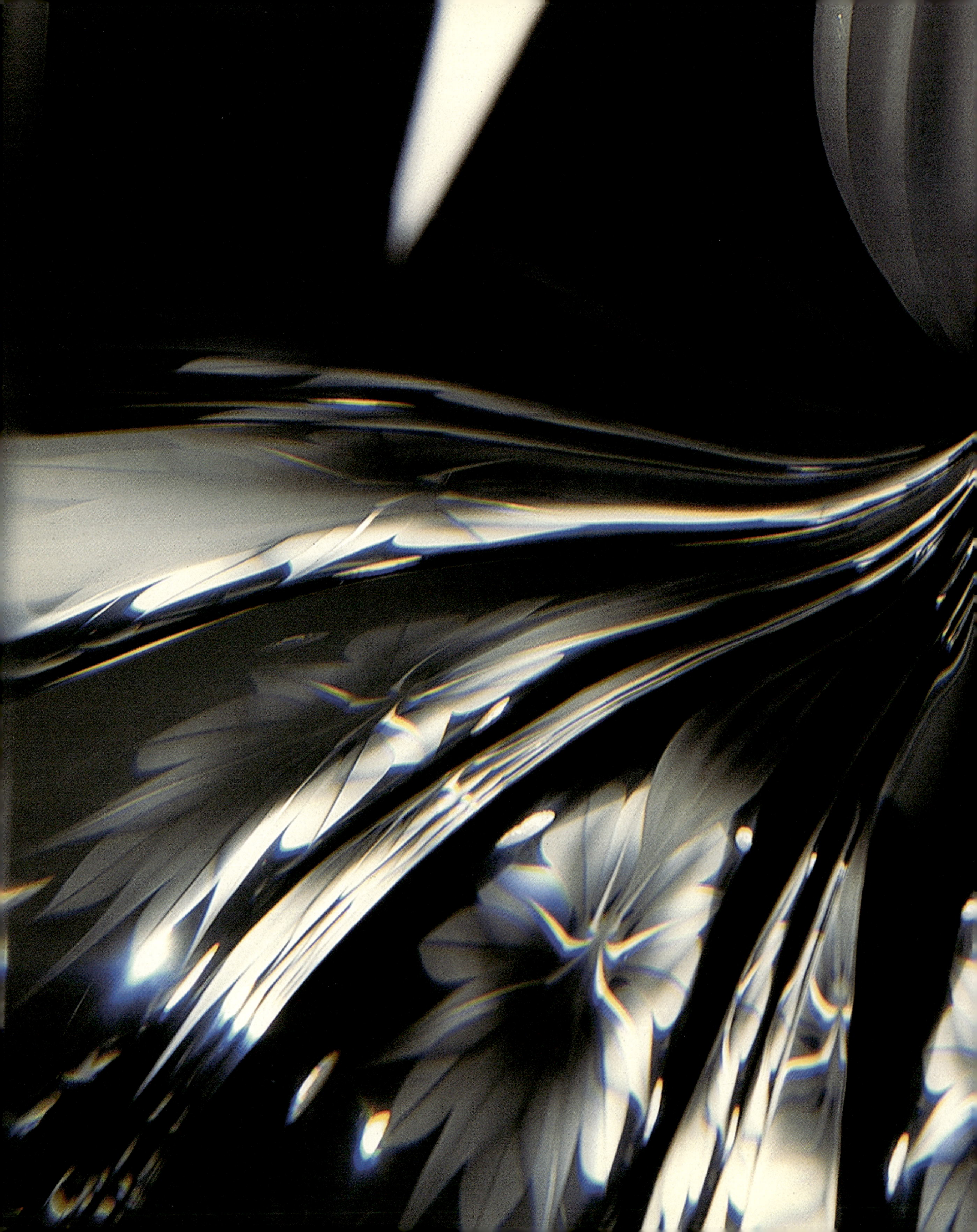

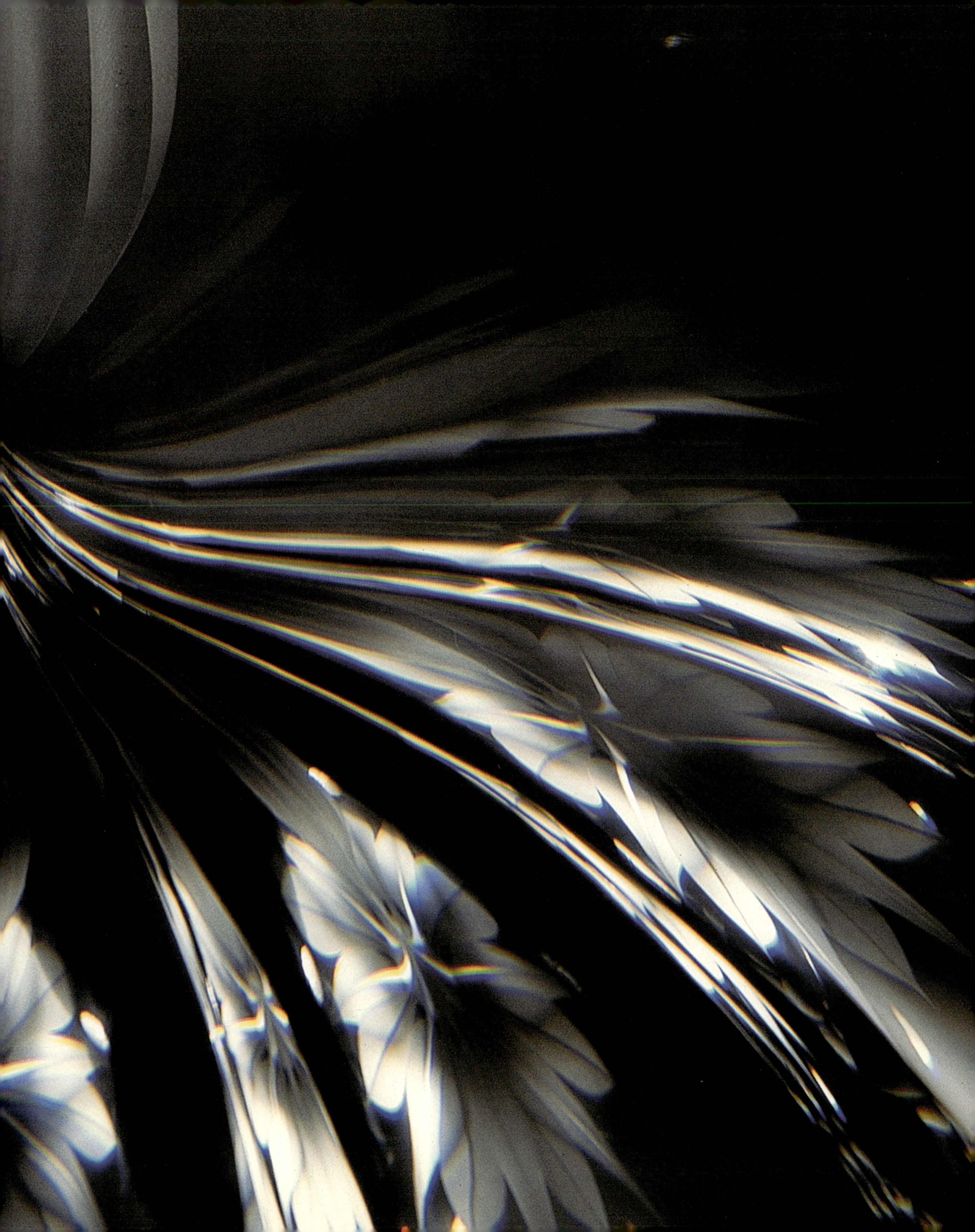

Cascade 1992

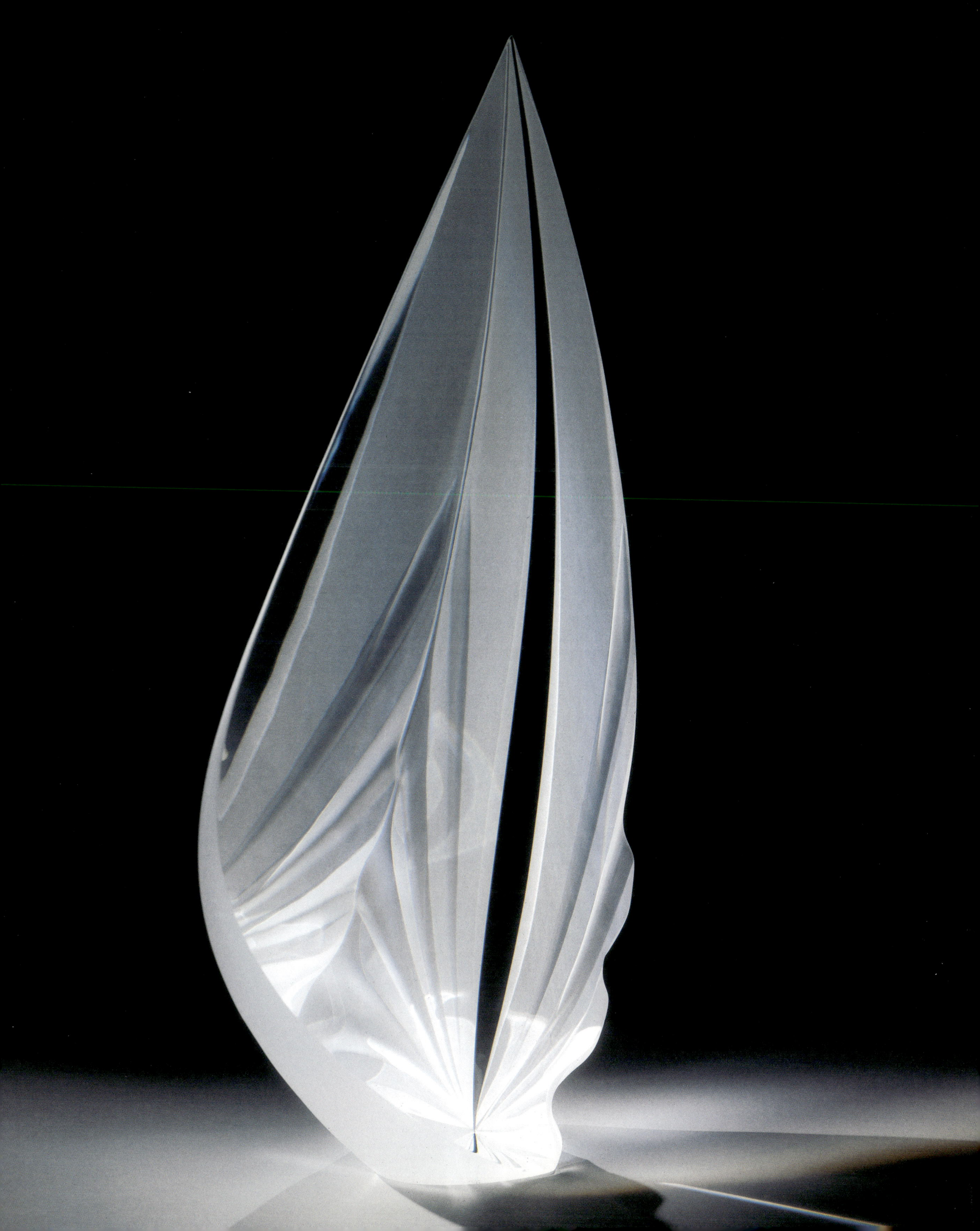

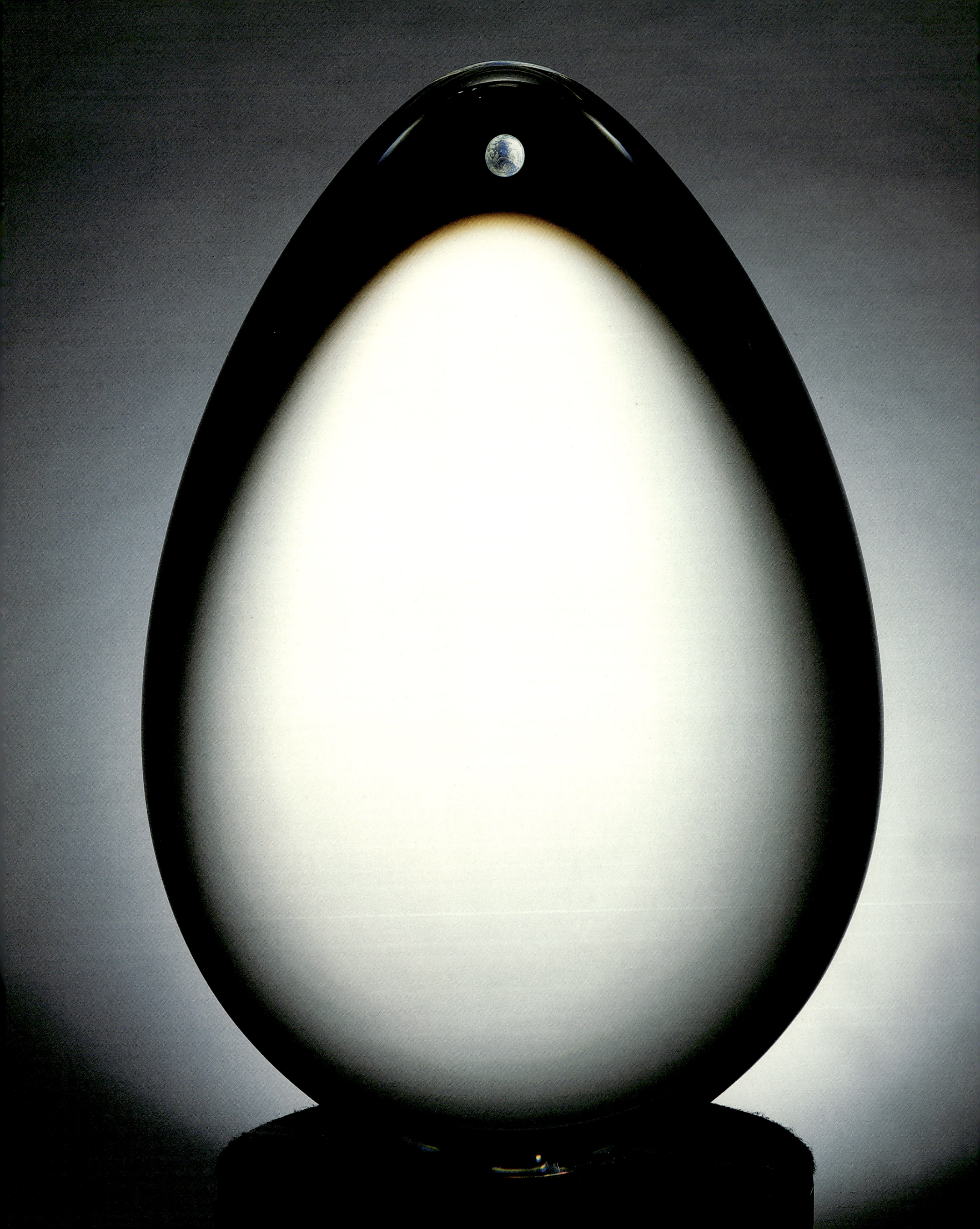

Life 1991

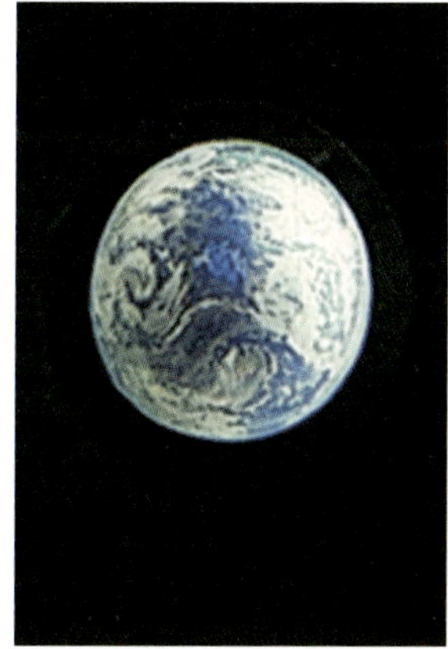

Lyric 1988

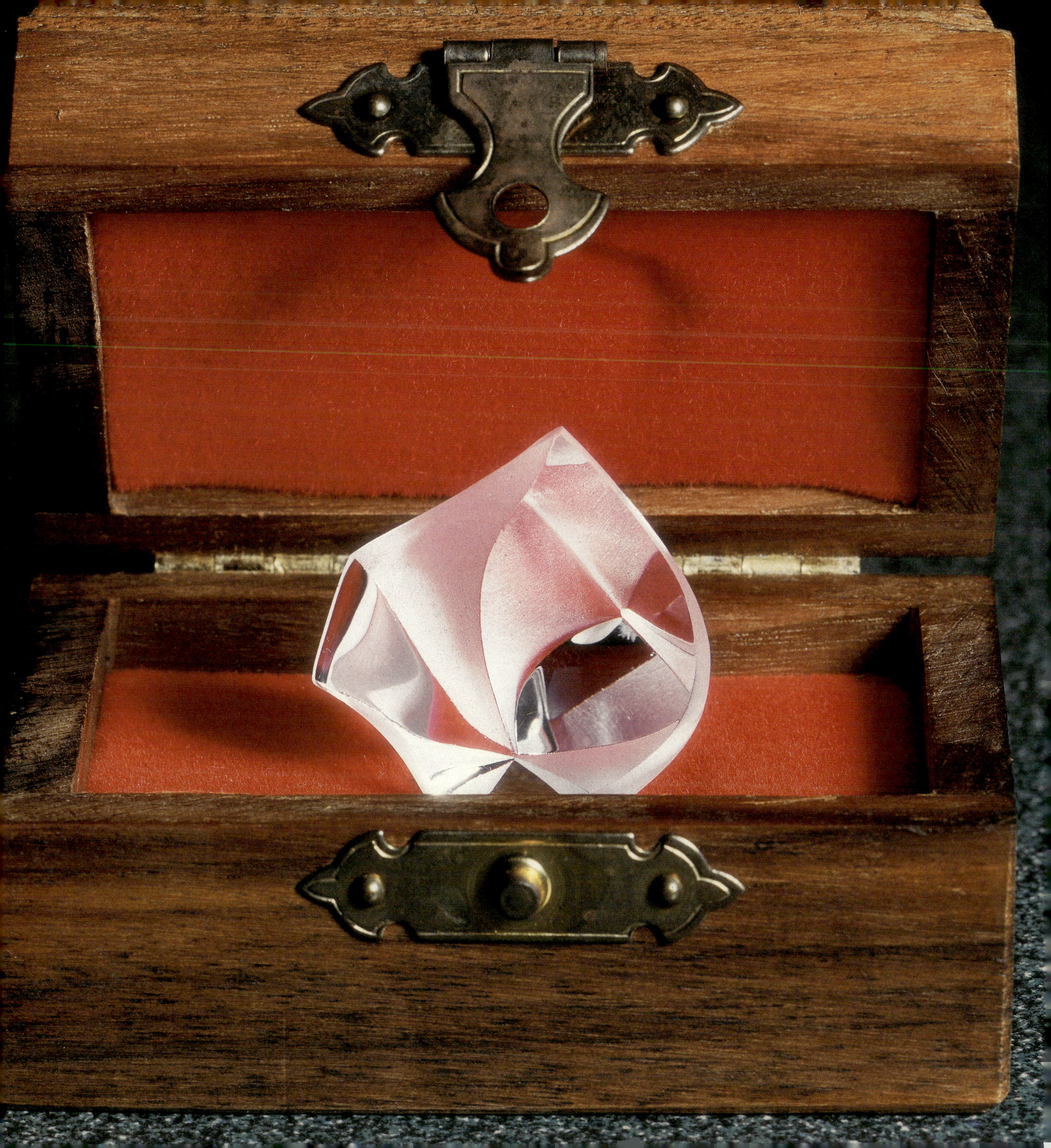

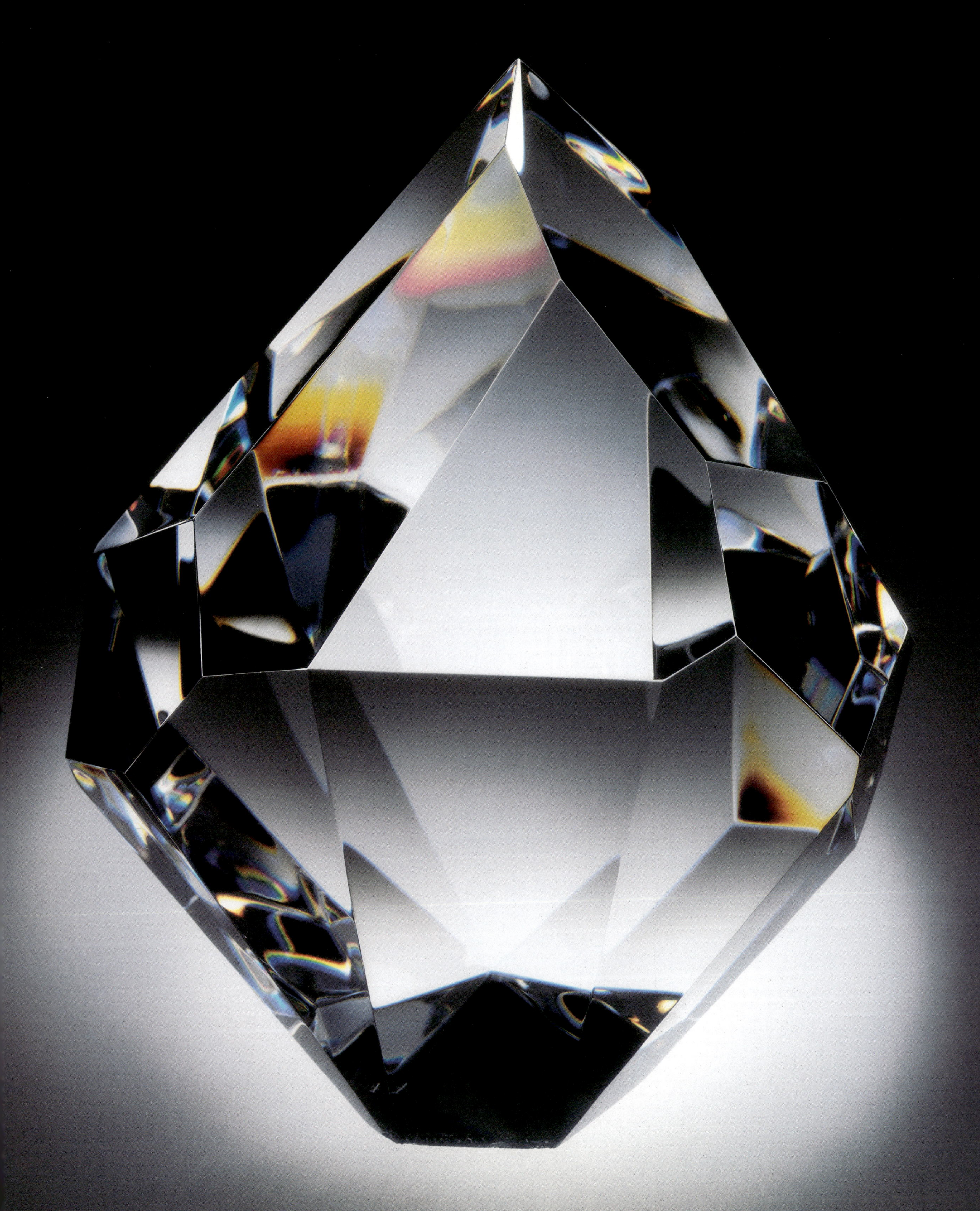

Harlequin 1988

Copper Cove 1986-87

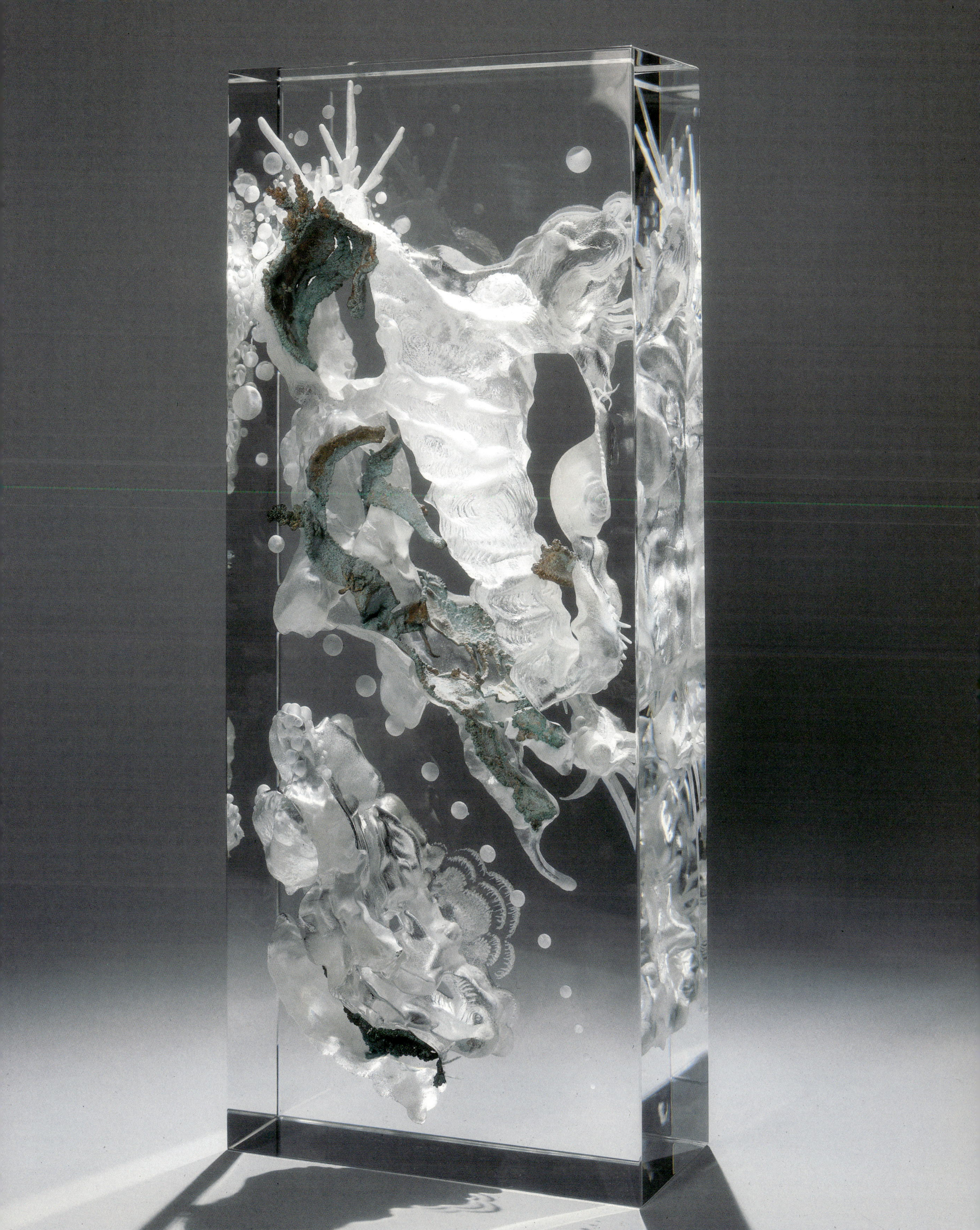

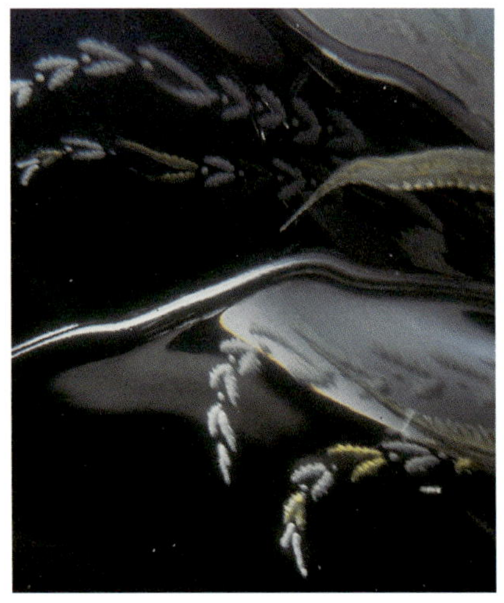

Bouquet 1983

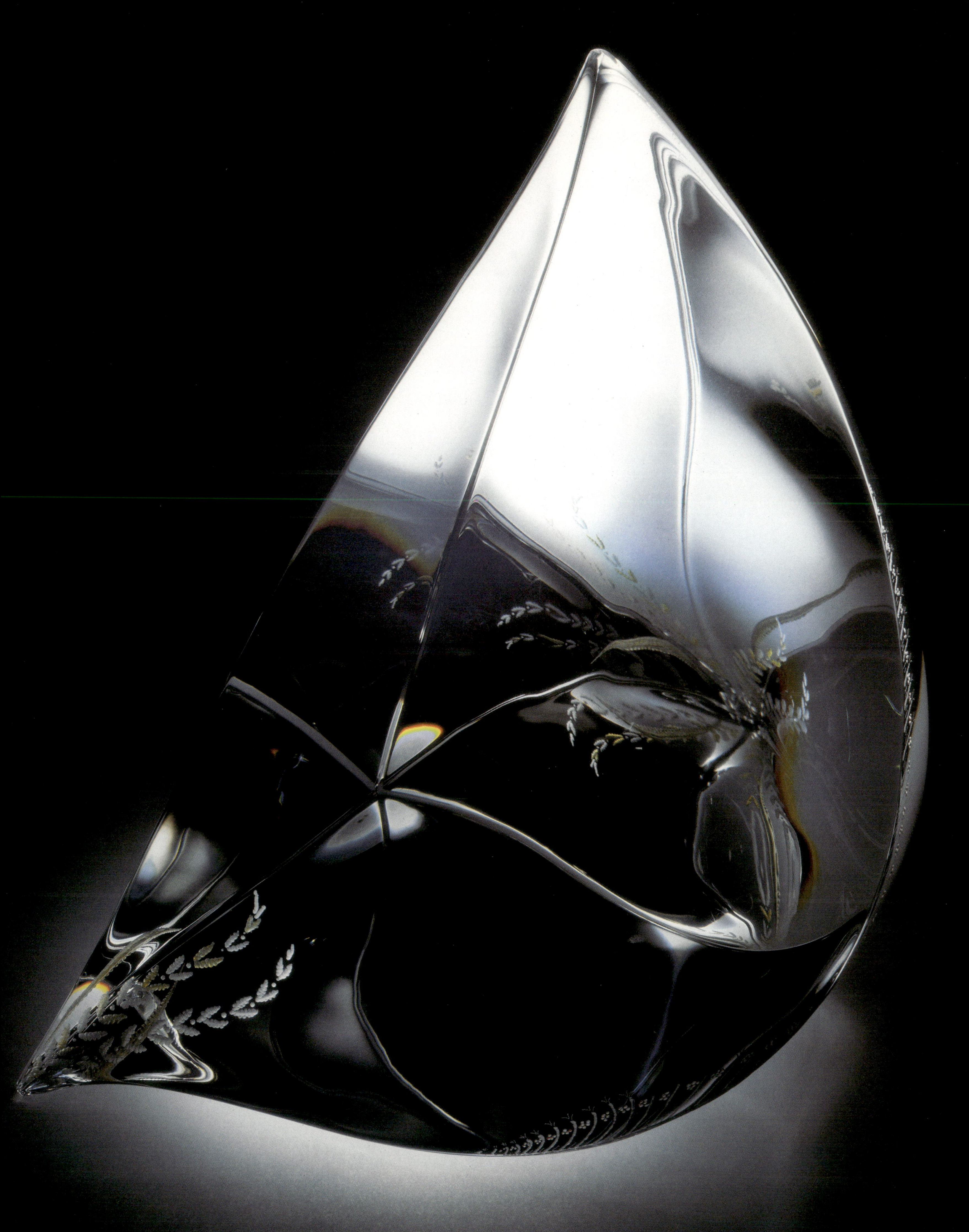

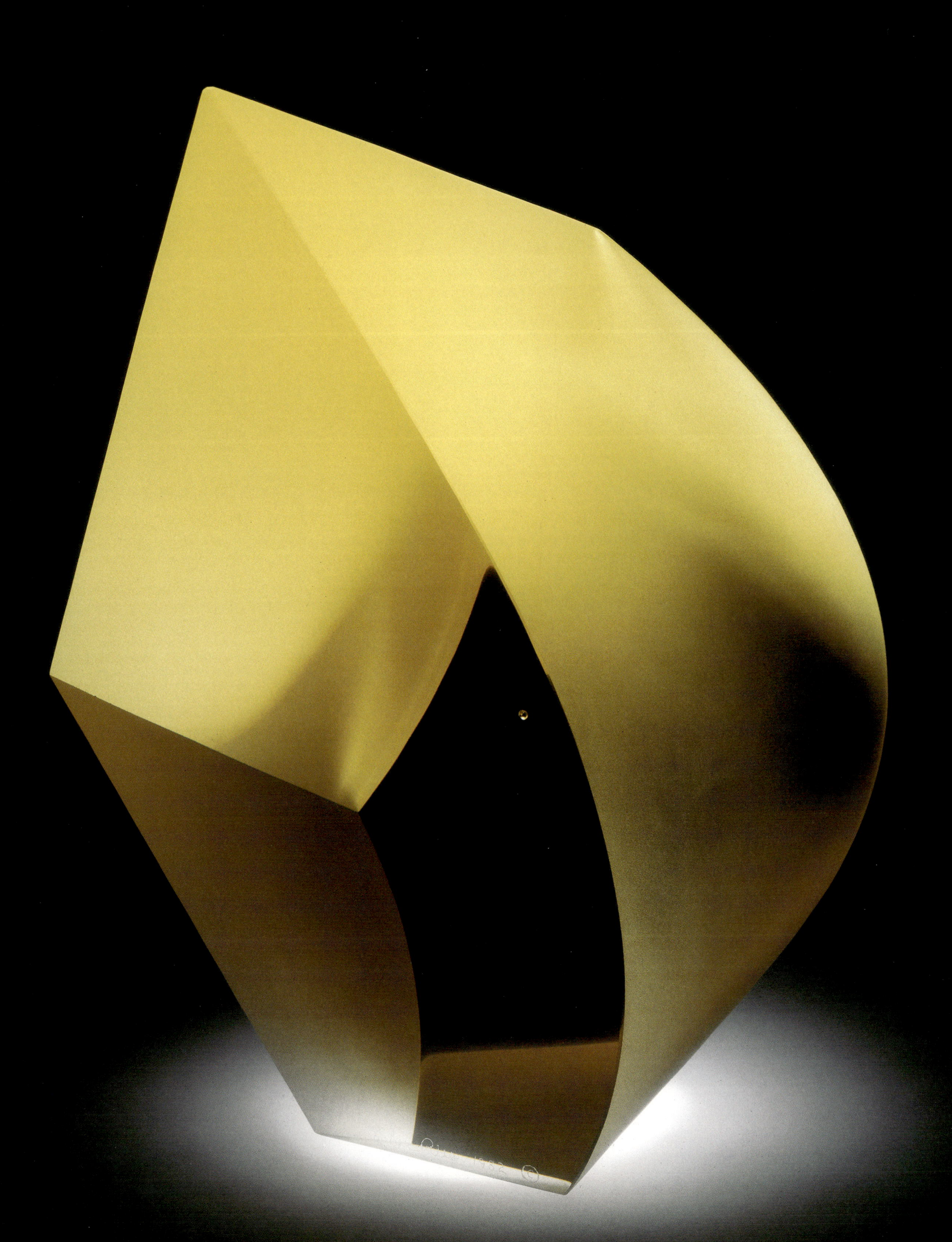

Solace 1982

Spider Engraving 1982

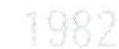

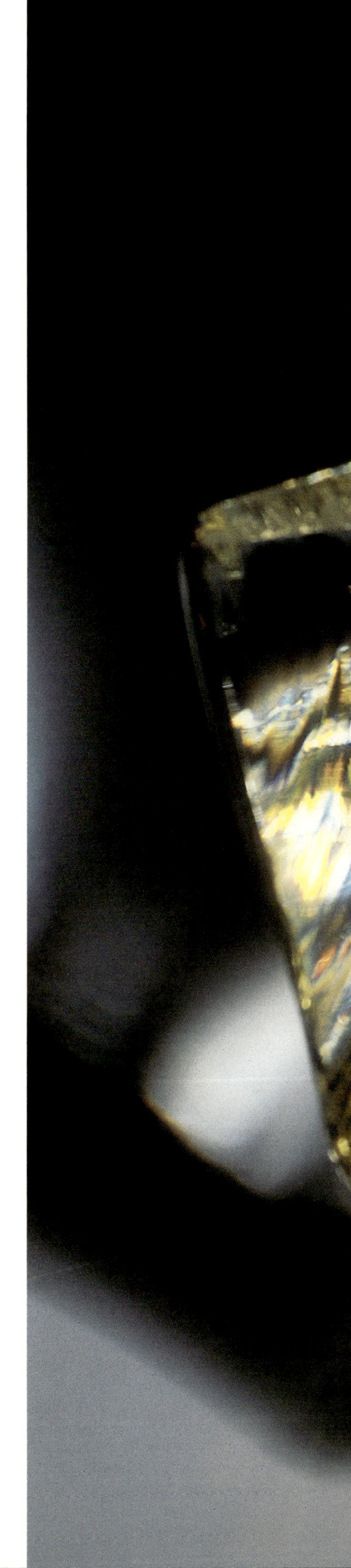

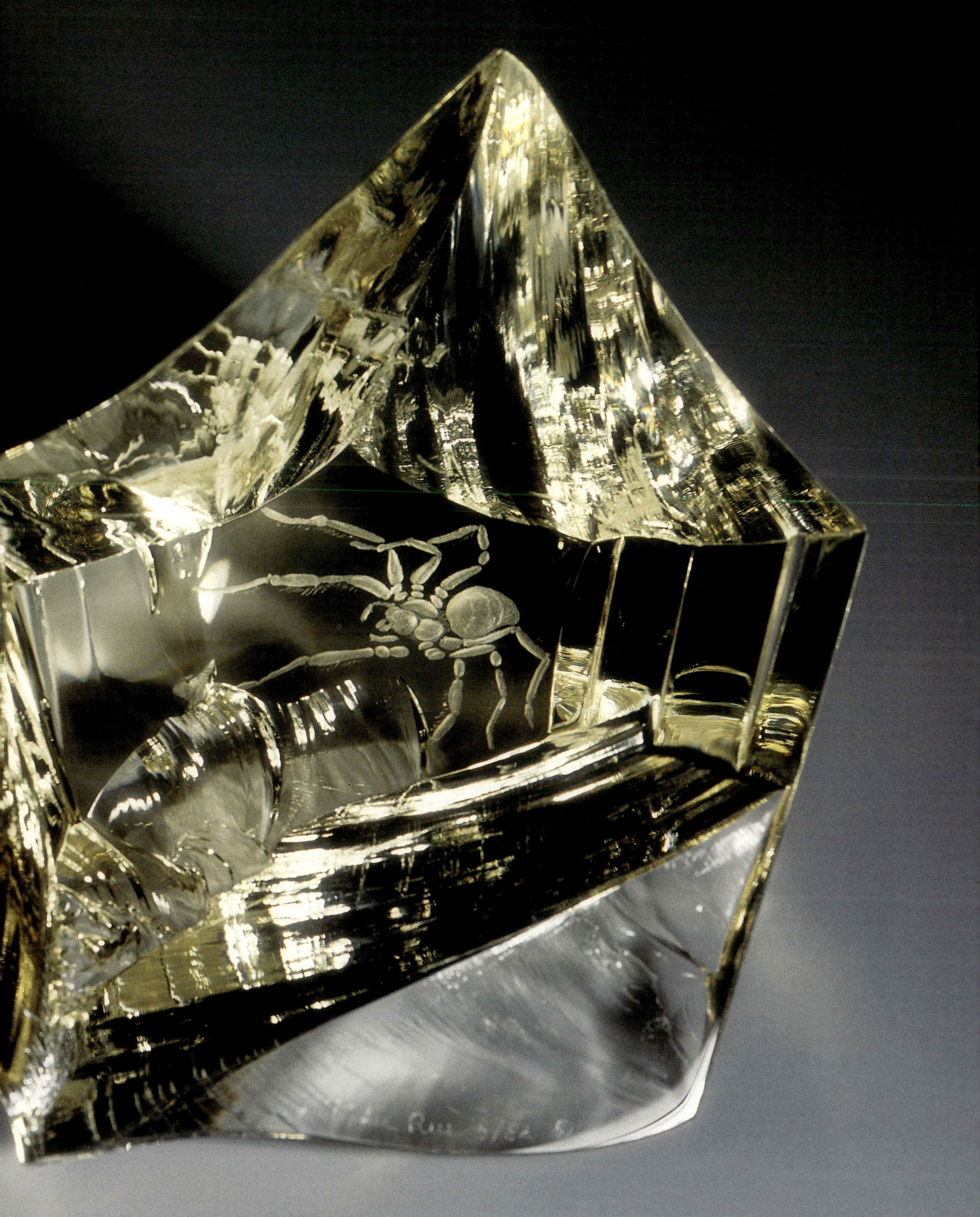

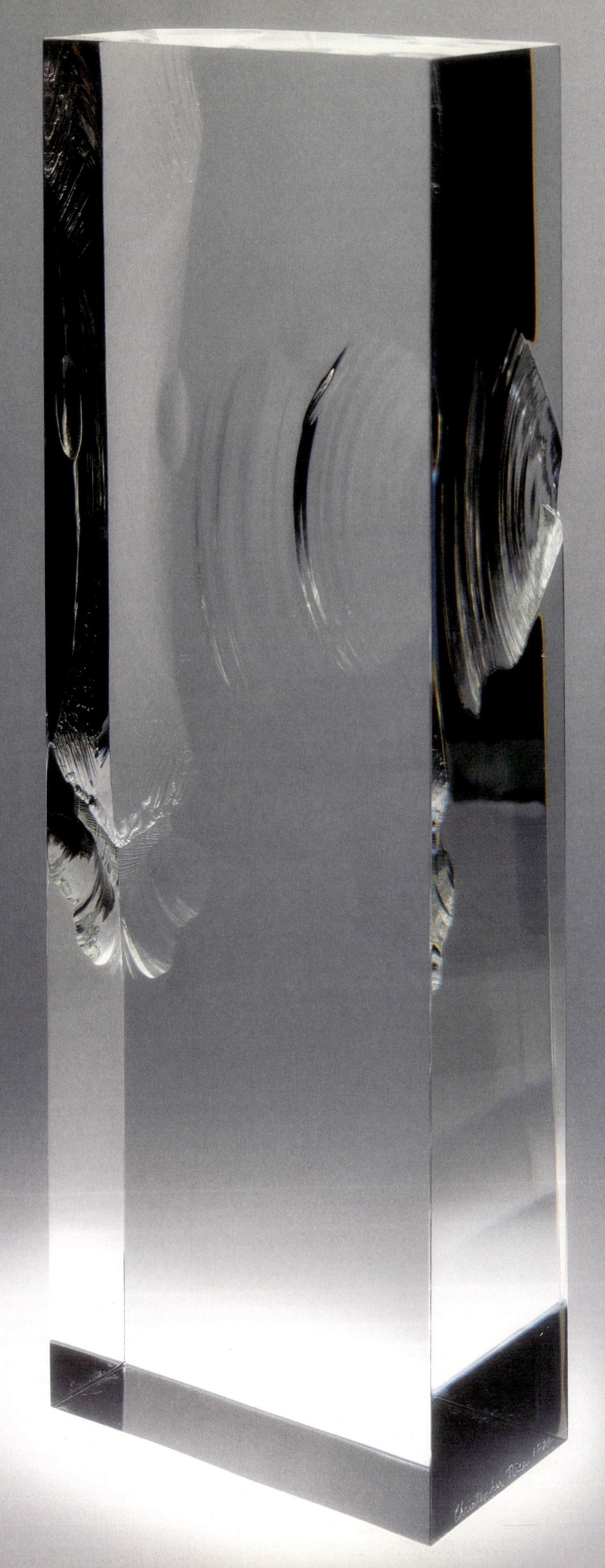

Wave in Space 1978

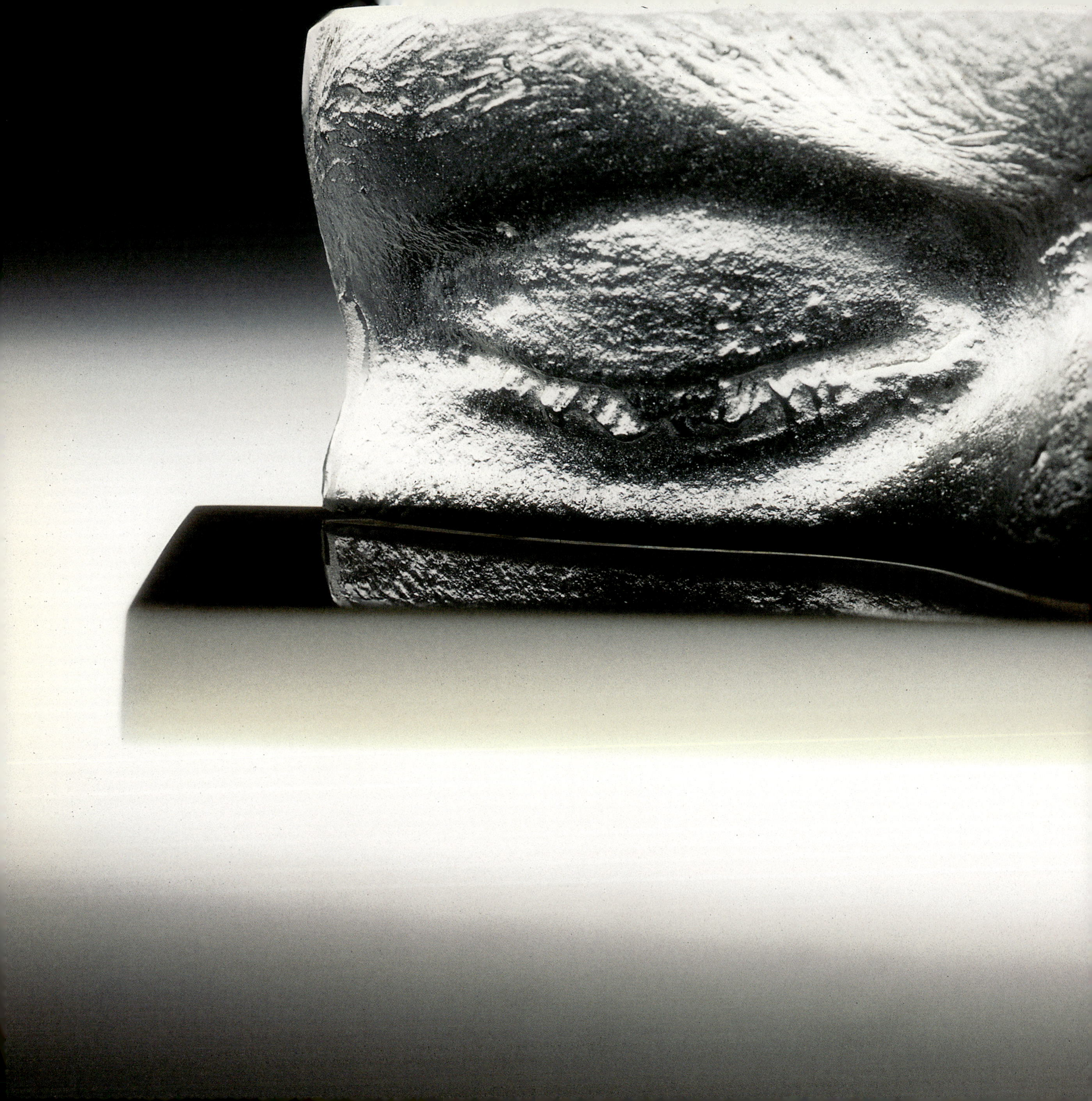

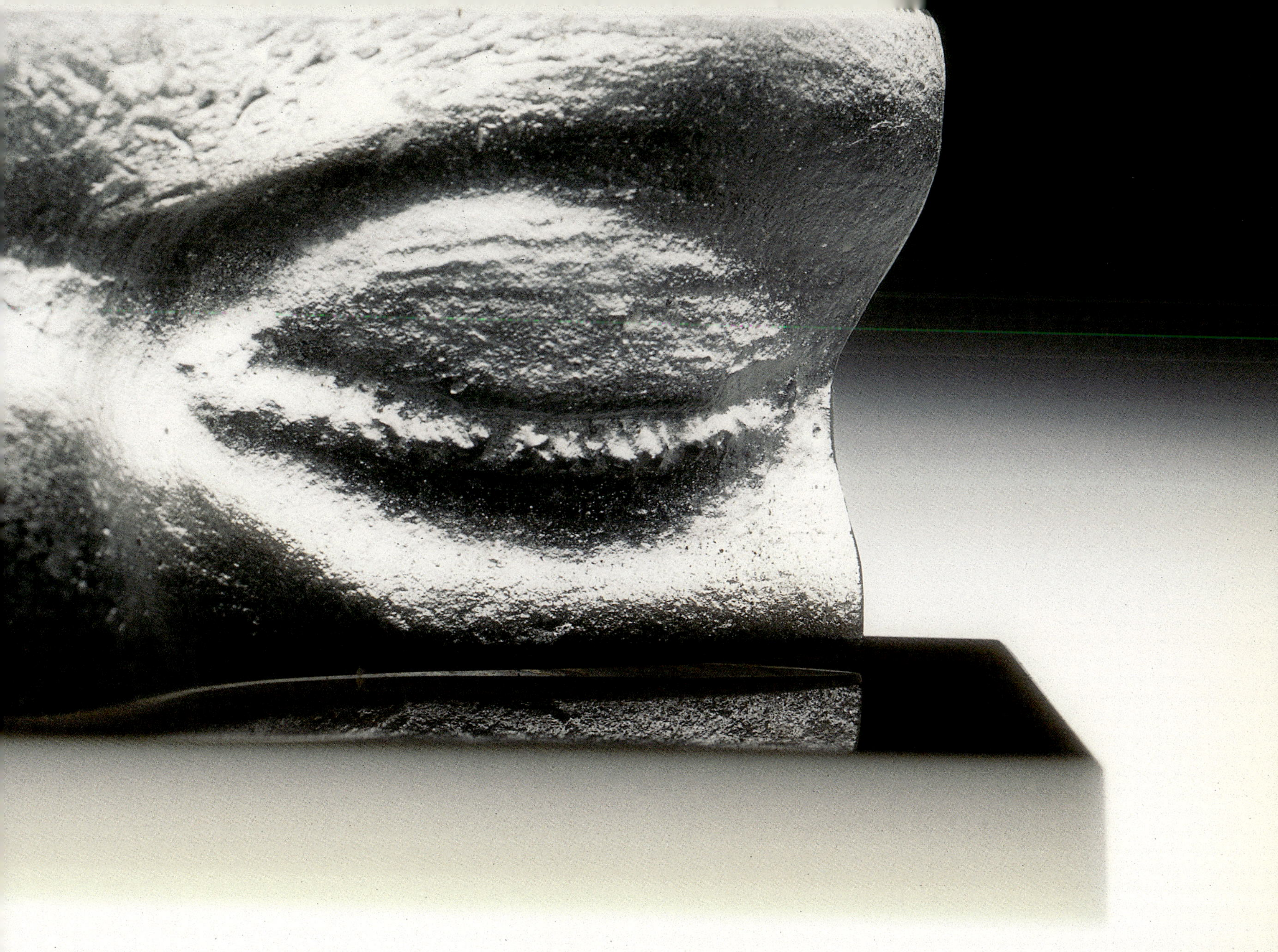

Artist's Life Mask 1976

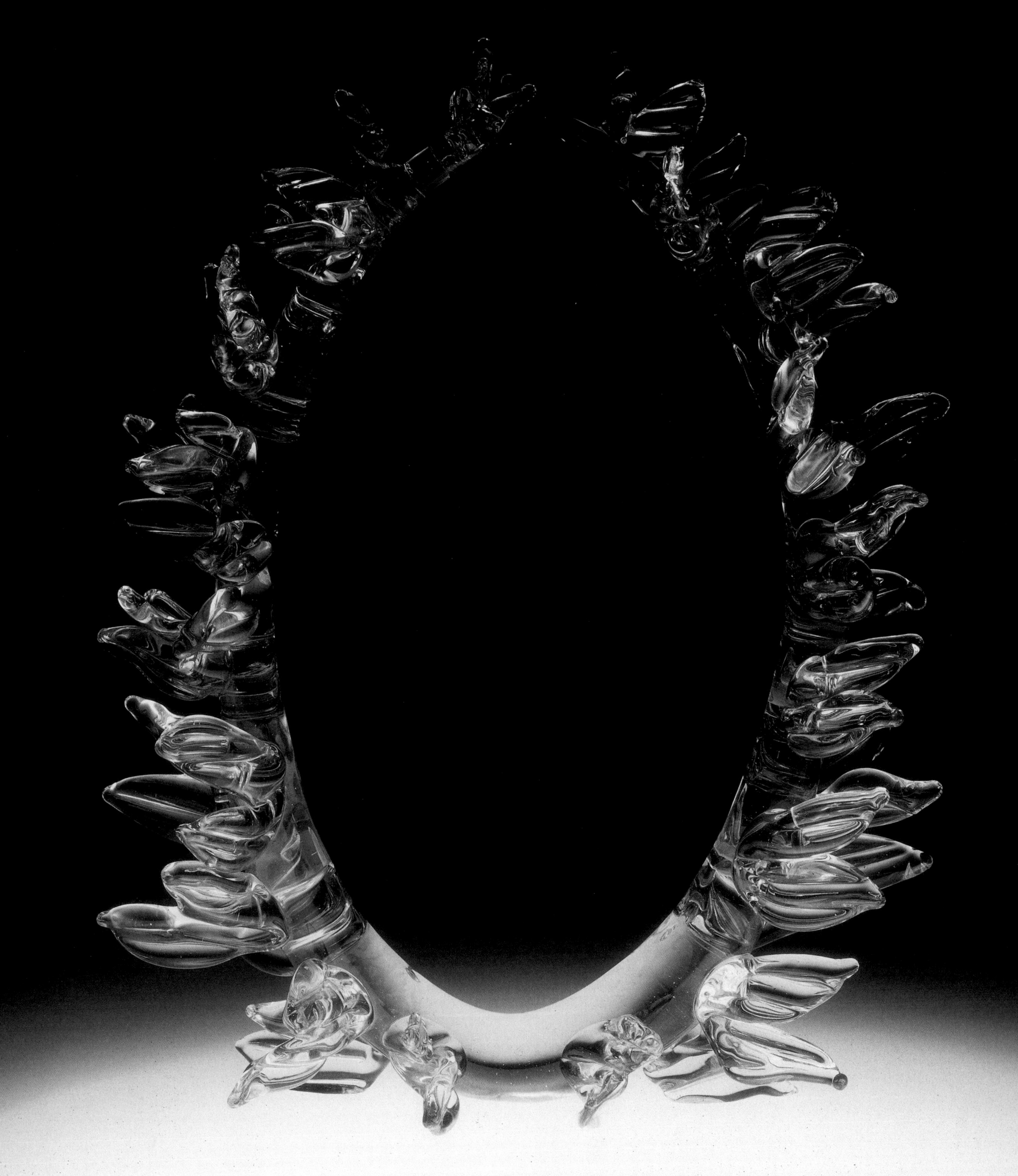

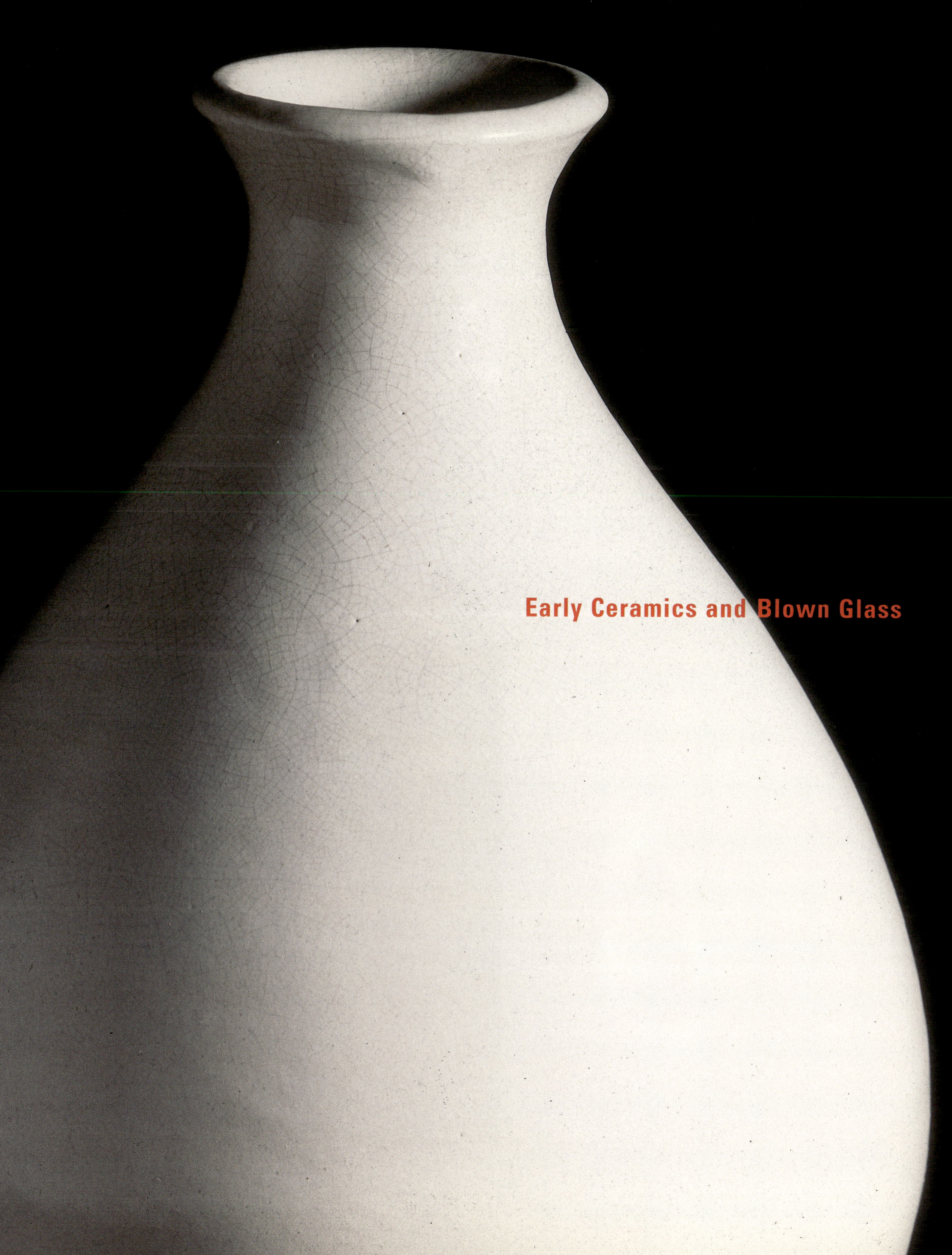

Early Ceramics and Blown Glass

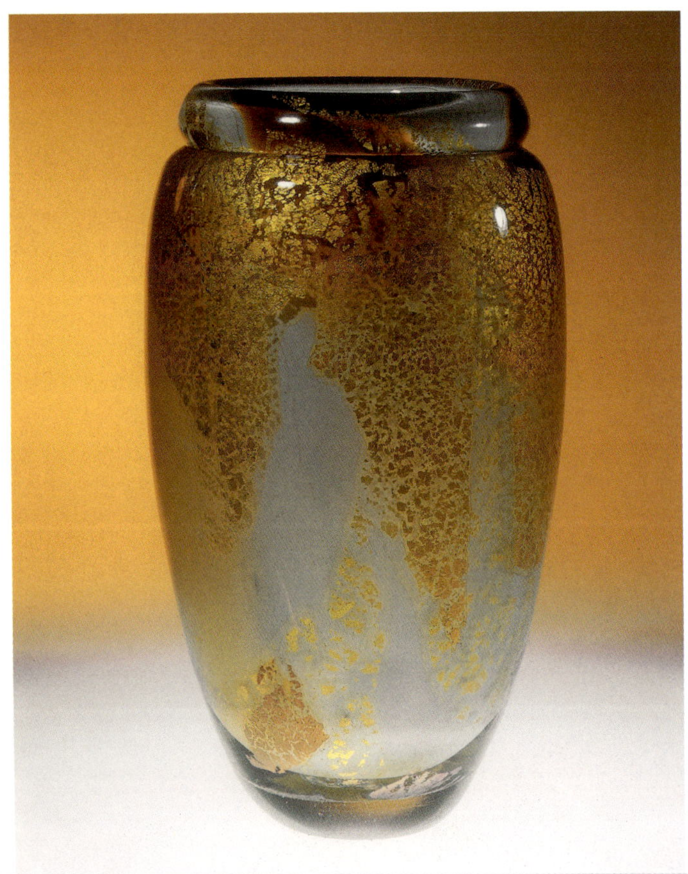

Vase 1979

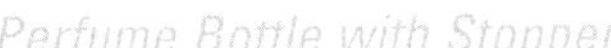

Perfume Bottle with Stopper 1979

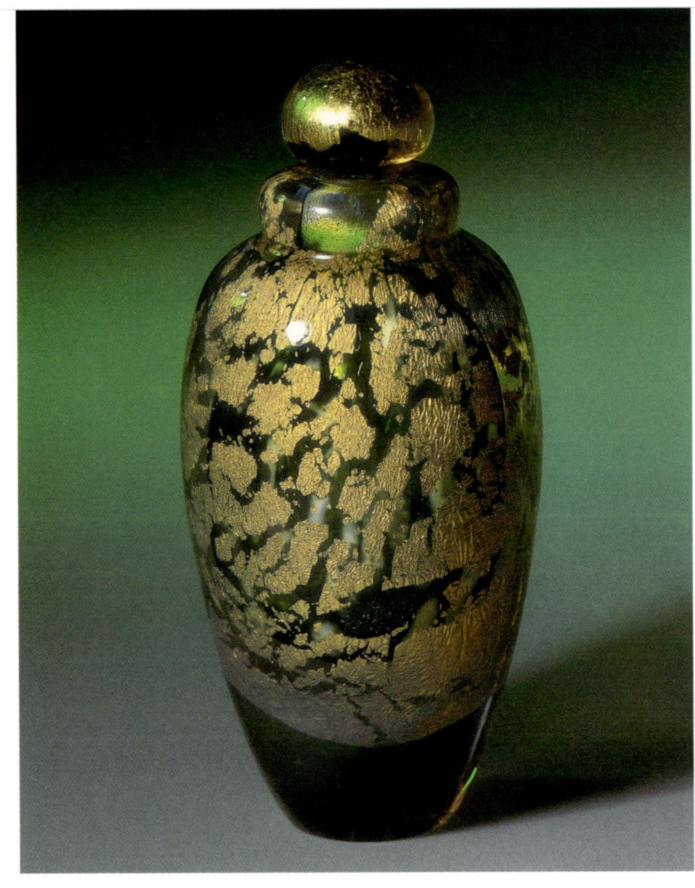

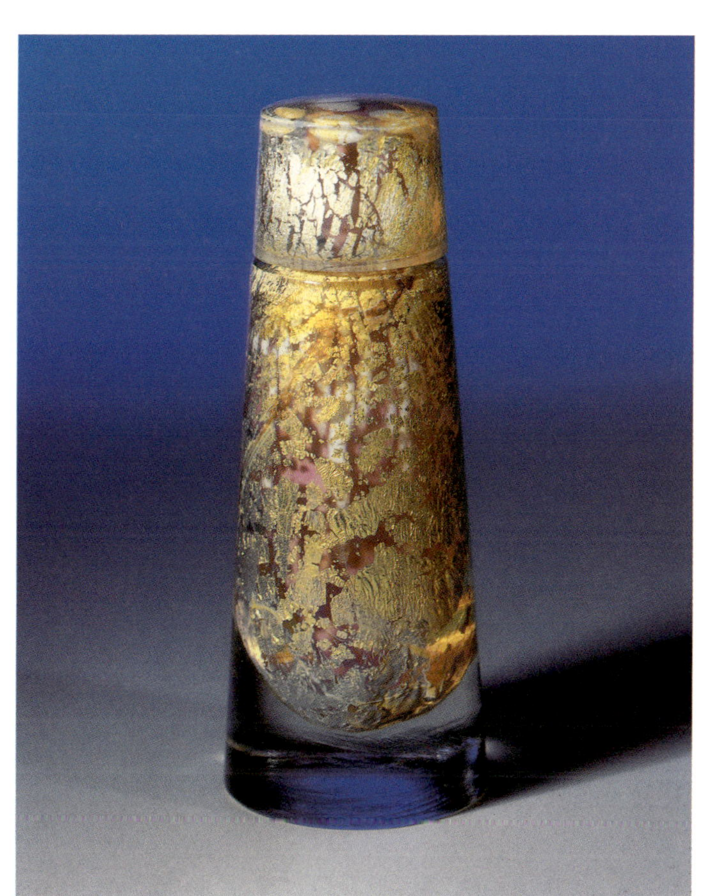

Perfume Bottle with Stopper 1978

Vase 1979

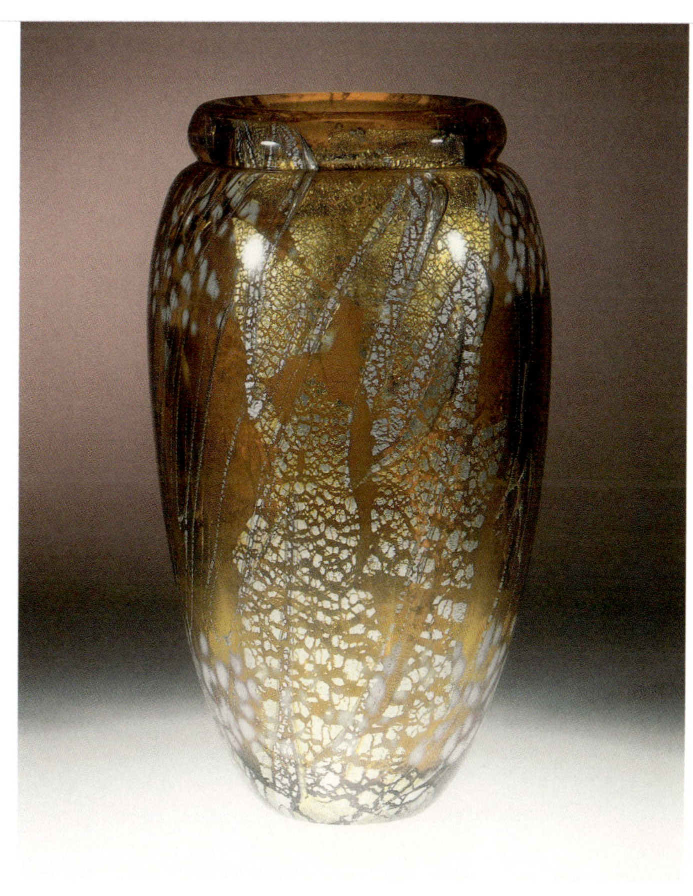

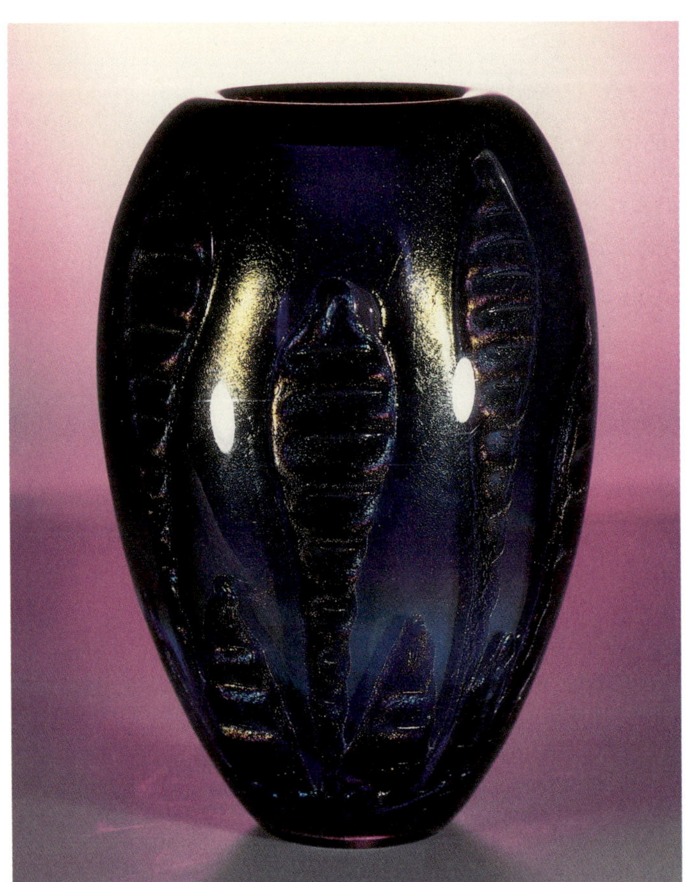

Vase 1978

Blown Bowl 1977

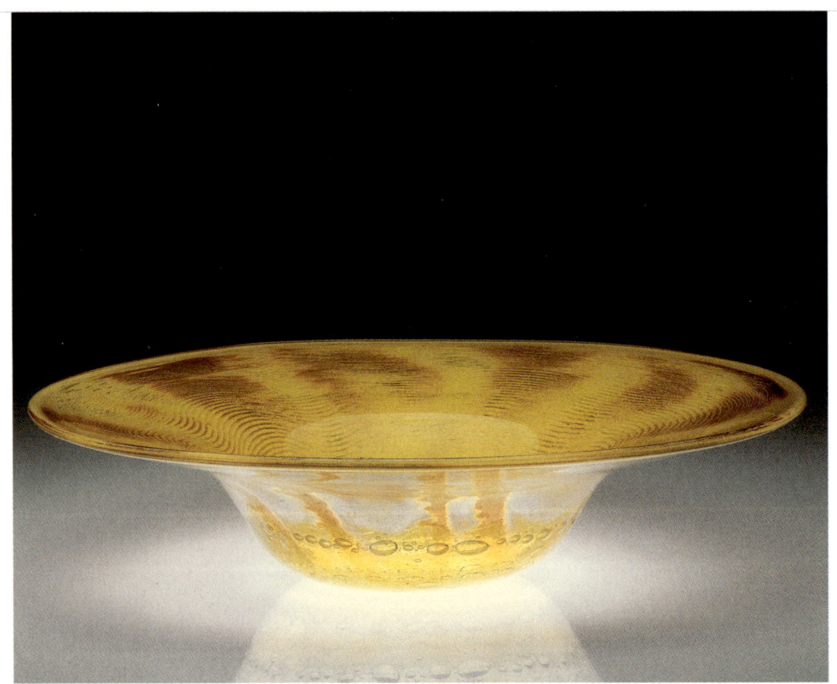

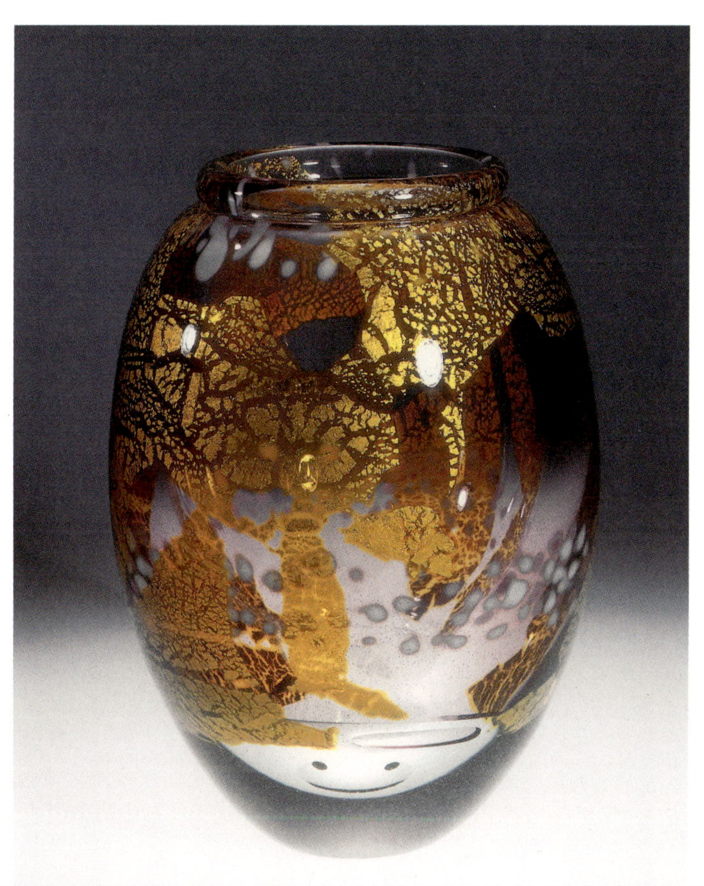

Vase 1977

Bowl 1977

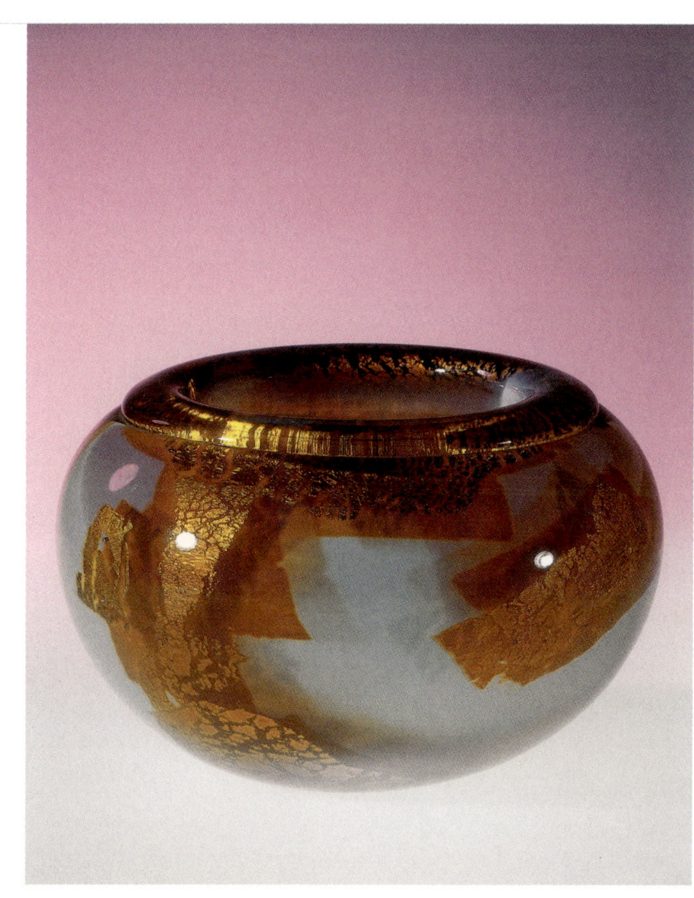

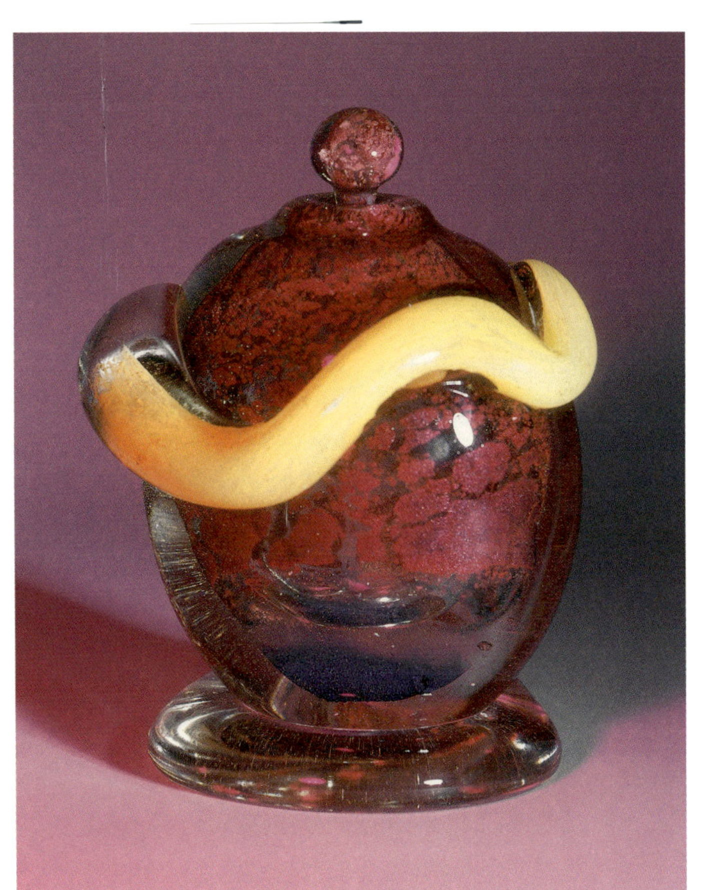

Perfume Bottle with Stopper 1976

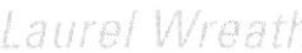

Laurel Wreath 1975

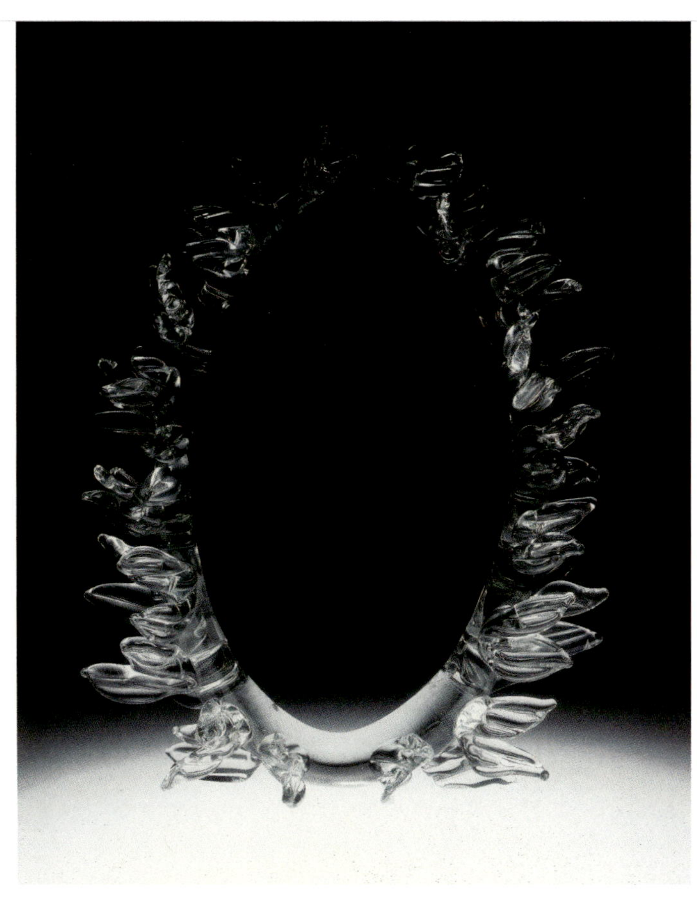

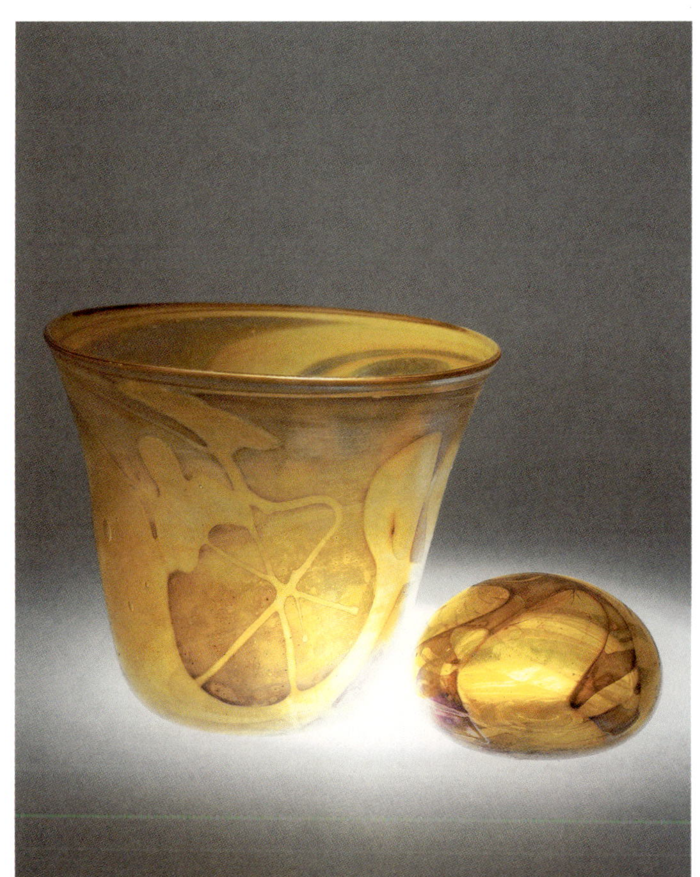

Vase and Paperweight 1975

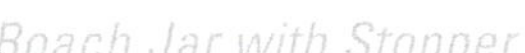

Roach Jar with Stopper 1975

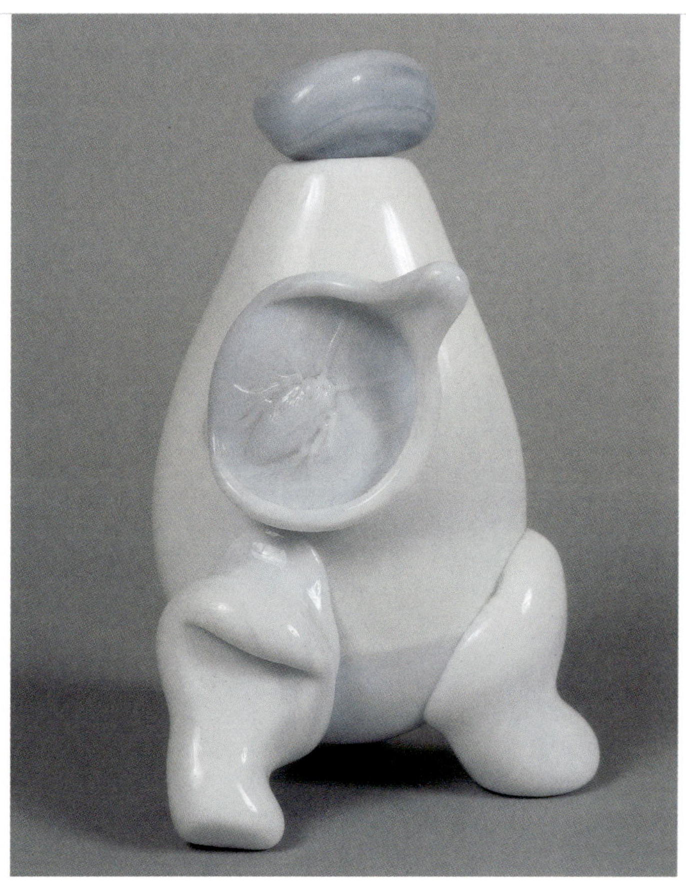

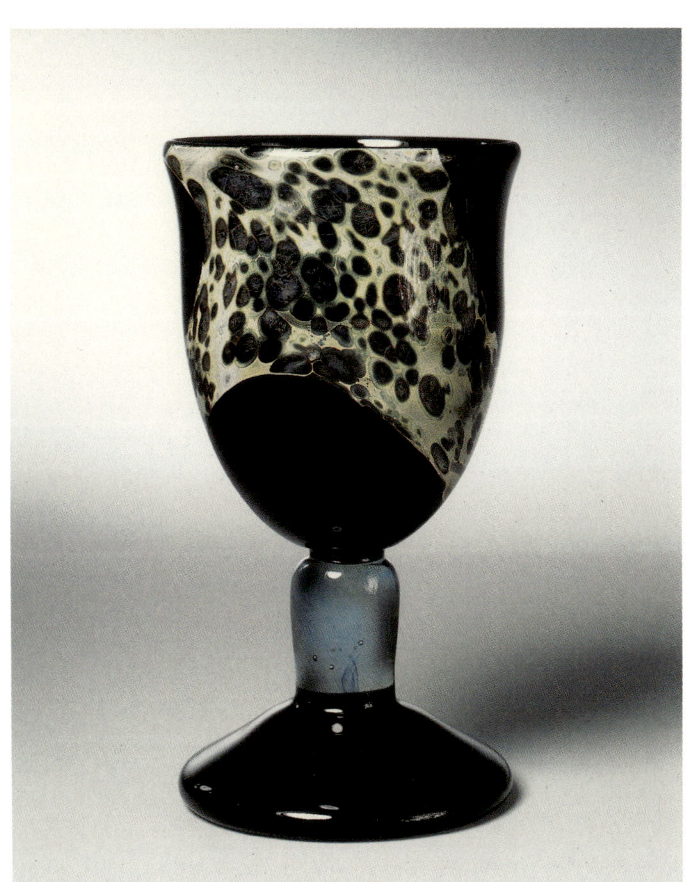

Goblet 1974

64

Vase 1973

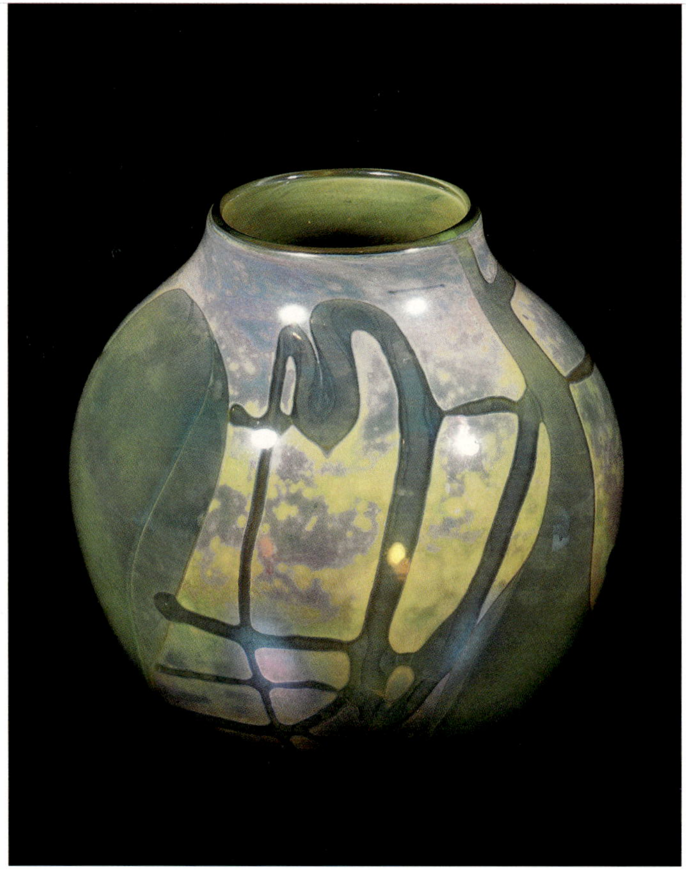

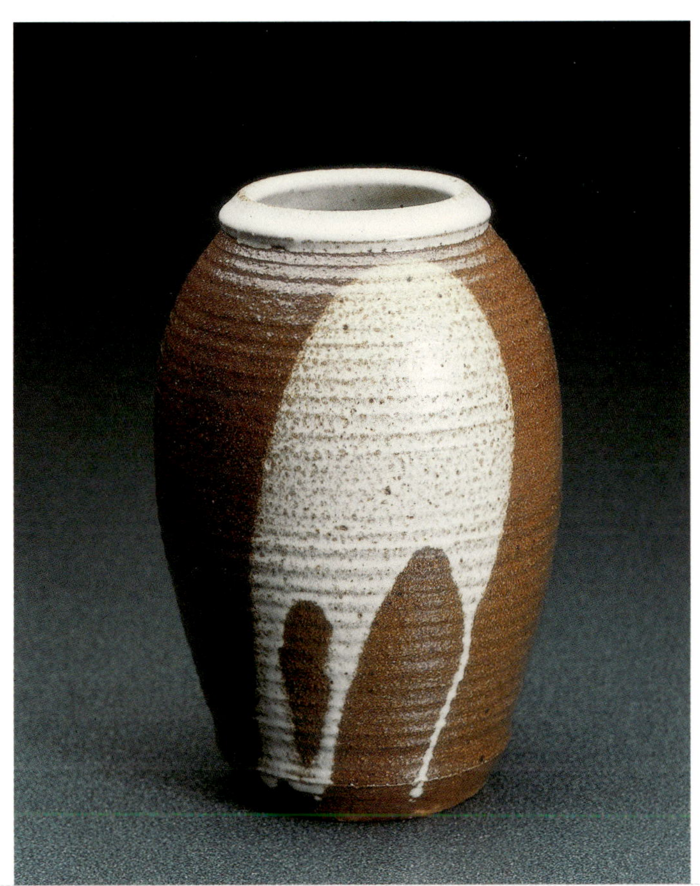

Vase 1972

Vase 1971

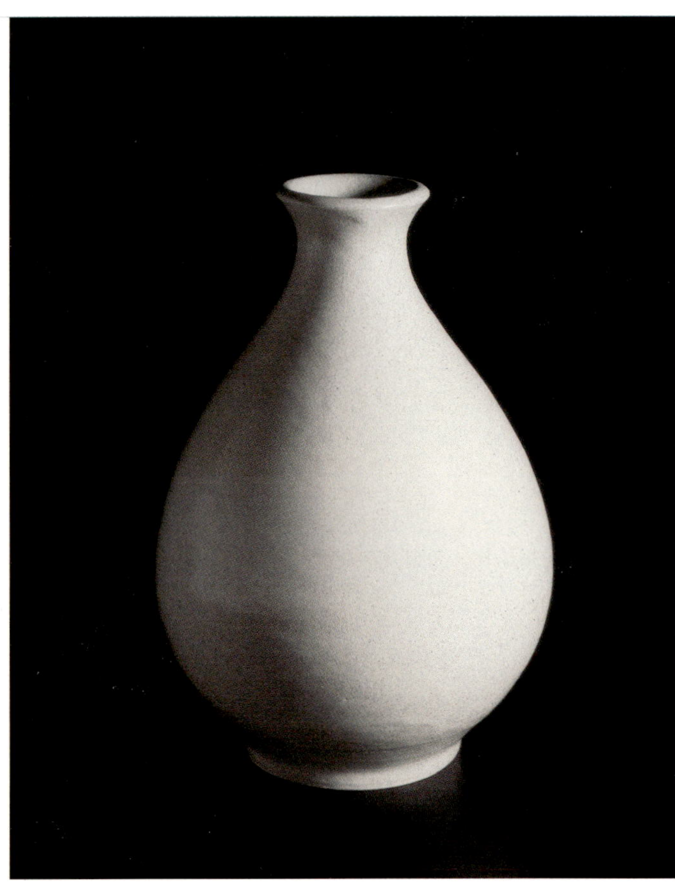

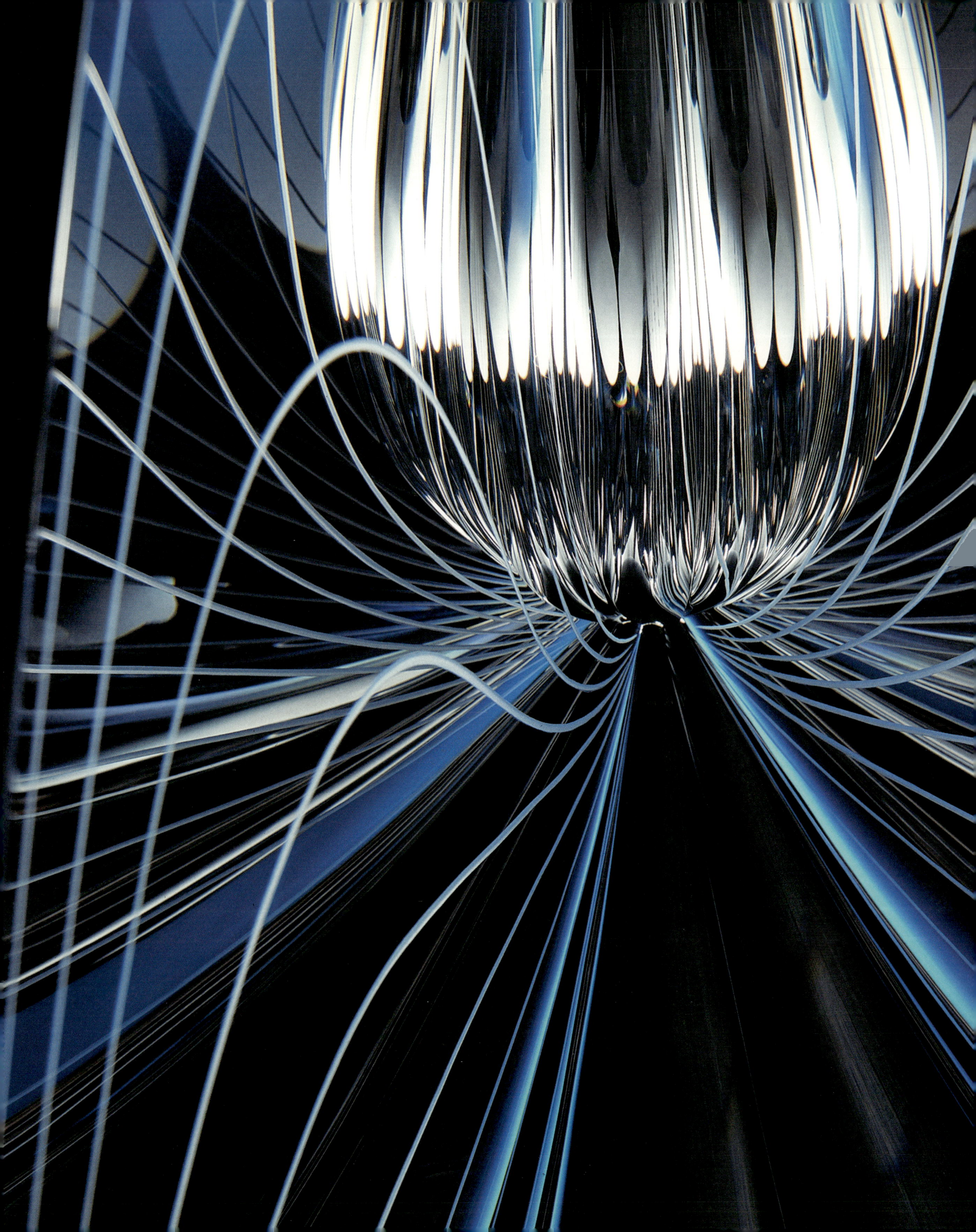

Checklist of the Exhibition

Carved Lead Crystal

1. *Falling Petals*, 2001
Optical lead crystal
37 3/4 x 18 1/4 x 8 3/4 in.; 186 lbs.
page 21

2. *Harp*, 2001
Optical lead crystal
31 7/8 x 19 1/2 x 8 in.; 103 lbs.
page 11, detail page 66

3. *Holiday*, 2001
Optical lead crystal
22 5/8 x 18 1/4 x 4 3/4 in.; 50 lbs.
page 18

4. *Blue Moon*, 2001
Optical glass
26 3/4 x 18 3/8 in.; 416 lbs.
page 6

5. *Embrace*, 2001
Optical lead crystal
41 3/4 x 22 3/4 x 7 1/4 in.; 351 lbs.
page 14

6. *Lotus*, 2001
Optical lead crystal
41 1/2 x 19 x 12 5/8 in.; 333 lbs.
page 17

7. *Spirit*, 2001
Optical lead crystal
37 1/8 x 12 1/8 x 8 3/8 in.; 161 lbs.
detail page 12

8. *Solstice*, 2001
Optical lead crystal
42 x 23 1/8 x 9 1/2 in.; 235 lbs.
Inside back flap, detail cover

9. *Bouquet of Light*, 2001
Optical lead crystal
43 3/8 x 23 1/4 x 10 in.; 291 lbs.
page 2, back cover, detail
inside covers

10. *Mezzo Luna*, 2000
Optical lead crystal
12 5/8 x 35 3/8 x 9 3/8 in.; 93 lbs.
page 23

11. *Point of View*, 1999
Optical lead crystal
27 1/2 x 38 1/2 x 8 in.; 213 lbs.
page 27, detail page 26

12. *Pacific Flora*, 1999
Optical lead crystal
32 3/4 x 12 2/8 x 7 5/8 in.; 84 lbs.
page 29

13. *Celebration*, 1999
Optical lead crystal
24 x 32 x 8 in.; 191 lbs.
pages 30-31

14. *Afterglow*, 1999
Optical lead crystal
41 1/4 x 28 3/4 x 14 in.; 513 lbs.
page 24

15. *Desert Flower*, 1996
Optical lead crystal
38 5/16 x 15 15/16 x 8 3/4 in.
(weight not available)
Collection of Dr. Ronald B.
and Jackie Carmen
page 32, detail pages 8-9, 33,
34-35

16. *Cascade*, 1992
Optical lead crystal
22 x 9 1/2 x 4 3/4 in.
(weight not available)
Private collection
page 37

17. *Life*, 1991
Optical lead crystal
33 5/8 x 22 1/4 in.; 1,041 lbs.
page 38

*18. *Harlequin*, 1988
Optical lead crystal; cut,
ground, and polished
7 7/8 x 7 x 4 in.
Private collection
page 42

19. *Lyric*, 1988
Optical lead crystal; cut,
ground, and polished
1 3/16 x 1 3/16 x 5/8 in.
page 41

20. *Copper Cove*, 1986-87
Optical lead crystal and pure copper;
cut, ground, polished, sandblasted, acid
etched, and diamond wheel engraved
18 1/4 x 7 1/2 x 3 1/4 in.
Columbus Museum of Art, Ohio:
Gift of Jay and Jill Orlip
page 45

21. *Bouquet*, 1983
Optical lead crystal; cut, ground,
polished, diamond wheel engraved,
and enameled
12 1/2 x 12 1/2 x 9 1/2 in.
Collection of Frank and Linda Kass
page 47

22. *Solace*, 1982
Optical lead crystal with cerium oxide
and entrapped bubble; cut, ground, and
polished, and 220 mesh grit texture
11 1/2 x 7 1/8 x 6 1/4 in.
Private collection
page 48

23. *Spider Engraving*, 1982
Naturally fractured glass with engraving
3 1/8 x 4 3/4 x 1 7/8 in.
pages 50-51

24. *Wave in Space*, 1978
Optical lead crystal with
natural fracture
15 1/2 x 5 1/8 x 3 3/4 in.
Columbus Museum of Art, Ohio:
A gift from Beaux Arts and friends
in memory of Nancy Howe Michael
and Marcia Walker Diwik
page 52

25. *Artist's Life Mask*, 1976
Cast crown glass; cut, ground,
and polished on Vitrolite base
1 7/16 x 4 3/8 x 1 3/4 in.
pages 54-55

** Weights not available for works dated 1988 and earlier.*

All works courtesy of the artist unless noted.

Early Ceramics and Blown Glass

26. *Vase*, 1979
Blown amber glass with silver leaf
and bit gathers, fumed with stannous
chloride and silver leaf cased in clear
glass, and ground and polished base
10 1/4 x 6 in.
page 59

27. *Vase*, 1979
Blown opal glass with gold leaf
and multiple casings, and ground
and polished base
11 1/2 x 6 5/8 in.
page 58

28. *Perfume Bottle With Stopper*, 1979
Blown chromium green glass with
gold leaf and bit gathers cased in
clear glass; cut, ground, and polished
7 7/8 x 3 7/8 in.
page 58

29. *Vase*, 1978
Blown cobalt blue glass with tooled
bit gathers, fumed with stannous
chloride and cased in clear glass,
and ground and polished base
8 11/16 x 5 7/8 in.
page 60

30. *Perfume Bottle With Stopper*, 1978
Blown opal glass with gold leaf and
white bit gathers cased in clear glass;
cut, ground, and polished
4 3/16 x 1 15/16 in.
page 59

31. *Vase*, 1977
Blown cranberry glass with white bit
gathers and gold leaf cased in clear
glass, and ground and polished base
9 1/4 x 6 3/4 in.
page 61

32. *Bowl*, 1977
Blown opal glass with gold leaf
cased in clear glass, and ground
and polished base
4 5/8 x 7 1/4 in.
page 61

33. *Blown Bowl*, 1977
Blown glass with combed enamels and
controlled patterned air bubbles
3 1/2 x 14 3/8 in.
page 60

34. *Perfume Bottle with Stopper*, 1976
Blown glass with powdered iron
and blue enamels and cased in clear
glass with applied trailing of yellow
enamel, applied foot, and ground and
polished base
5 11/16 x 3 13/16 x 3 1/8 in.
page 62

35. *Laurel Wreath*, 1975
Hot-worked glass bits made
on puntil rod
10 1/2 x 7 3/4 x 3 in.
pages 56, 62

36 & 37. *Vase and Paperweight*, 1975
Blown glass with silver nitrate and
stannous chloride
5 1/2 x 6 1/2 in.; 2 1/2 x 4 1/2 in.
Collection of Jack and Janice Roth
page 63

38. *Roach Jar with Stopper*, 1975
Blown white opaline Fenton glass
with applied and stamped bits
9 x 5 1/4 x 4 1/2 in.
Collection of Jack and Janice Roth
page 63

39. *Goblet*, 1974
Blown black glass with silver nitrate,
marvered frit and bit gathers, and
applied stem and foot
6 1/2 x 3 1/4 in.
page 64

40. *Vase*, 1973
Blown glass from remelted Pepsi
bottles with silver nitrate surface
decoration and trailed over with
clear glass
8 3/8 x 8 in.
page 64

41. *Vase*, 1972
Hand thrown stoneware with salt glaze
10 x 6 1/2 in.
page 65

42. *Vase*, 1971
Hand thrown, white earthenware
with commercial glaze
7 1/4 x 5 1/16 in.
page 65, detail page 57

All works collection of the artist unless noted.

Christopher Ries, b. 1952

Lives and works in Tunkhannock, Pennsylvania

EDUCATION

1975 Bachelor of Fine Arts in ceramics and glass, The Ohio State University, Columbus, Ohio.

1978 Master of Fine Arts in glass, University of Wisconsin, Madison, Wisconsin.

ONE PERSON EXHIBITIONS

2001
The Glass Sculpture of Christopher Ries, The Columbus Museum of Art, Columbus, Ohio.

Riley Hawk Galleries, Columbus, Ohio. Also 1999, 1998, 1996, 1995, 1993, 1992, 1991, 1989.

2000
Christopher Ries Crystal, Old State House, Hartford, Connecticut.

The Rachael Collection, Aspen, Colorado. Also 1998, 1996.

1999
Christopher Ries: Sculpture of Glass, Lore Degenstein Gallery, Susquehanna University, Selinsgrove, Pennsylvania.

Merrill Chase Galleries, Chicago, Illinois. Also 1997.

1998
Illusions of Light: The Glass Sculpture of Christopher Ries, York College Galleries, York, Pennsylvania.

Miller Gallery, Cincinnati, Ohio. Also 1993, 1991, 1988, 1985.

1997
Riley Hawk Galleries, Cleveland, Ohio. Also 1995, 1992, 1991, 1989.

1996
Crystal Illusions: The Sculpture of Christopher Ries, Bergstrom-Mahler Museum, Neenah, Wisconsin.

Glass & Light: The Sculpture of Christopher Ries, Everhart Museum, Scranton, Pennsylvania.

Whitt/Krauss Objects of Fine Art, Palm Desert, California.

Naples Art Gallery, Naples, Florida. Also 1995.

1995
Glas und Licht: Skulpturen von Christopher Ries, Südwest Funk Gallerie, Mainz, Germany.

Optical Illusions: Glass Sculpture by Christopher Ries, Headley-Whitney Museum, Lexington, Kentucky.

Heike Pickett Gallery, Lexington, Kentucky.

1993
The Sculpture of Christopher Ries, The Winter Garden, PPG Industries, Pittsburgh, Pennsylvania.

LaFond Galleries, Pittsburgh, Pennsylvania. Also 1992.

1992
Bell Gallery, Memphis, Tennessee.

1990
Christopher Ries REFLECTIONS: An Exhibition of Glass Sculpture, Contemporary Gallery, Marywood University, Scranton, Pennsylvania.

1988
Illusions in Glass: The Art of Christopher Ries, Cincinnati Art Museum, Cincinnati, Ohio.

Christopher Ries: Miracles in Optic Glass, Zanesville Art Center, Zanesville, Ohio.

1987
Gallery 200, Columbus, Ohio. Also 1985, 1982, 1980.

1985
Barrett Gallery, Toledo, Ohio.

Prescott Gallery, Santa Fe, New Mexico.

1984
Habatat Gallery, Pontiac, Michigan.

1981
Marilyn Faith Gallery, Chicago, Illinois.

The Glass Art Gallery, Toronto, Canada. Also 1980.

Galleria of Sculpture, Palm Beach, Florida.

1980
Contemporary Art Glass Group, New York, New York. Also 1979.

GROUP EXHIBITIONS

2001
Treasures for a Queen: A Millennium Gift to Cincinnati, Cincinnati Art Museum, Cincinnati, Ohio.

New Faces in Glass, Gallery 500, Elkins Park, Pennsylvania.

Glass Weekend, Wheaton Village, Millville, New Jersey. (Symposium/ Exhibition) Also 1999, 1997, 1995, 1993, 1991, 1989.

2001 continued
Palm Springs Art Fair, Palm Springs, California.

A Touch of Glass, Cincinnati Art Museum, Cincinnati, Ohio.

2000
Sculpture Objects and Functional Art (SOFA) Exposition, Chicago, Illinois. Also 1999, 1998, 1997, 1996, 1995, 1994.

Kunst Rai, Rai Congrescentrum, Amsterdam, The Netherlands. Also 1997, 1996.

Old Statehouse, Hartford, Connecticut. Also 1989.

1999
Clearly Inspired: Contemporary Glass and Its Origins, Tampa Museum of Art, Tampa, Florida.

Art Palm Beach, West Palm Beach, Florida.

Buschlen Mowatt Fine Arts, Ltd., Vancouver, Canada.

1998
Gerald Peters Gallery, Santa Fe, New Mexico.

Holsten Gallery, Stockbridge, Massachusetts. Also 1994, 1993.

1997
Glass Today: American Studio Glass from Cleveland Collections, Cleveland Museum of Art, Cleveland, Ohio.

Sculpture Objects and Functional Art (SOFA) Exposition, Miami, Florida. Also 1996, 1995.

Naples Art Gallery, Naples, Florida. Also 1993, 1992.

1996
Gallery Lara, Chicago, Illinois.

Merrill Chase Galleries, Chicago, Illinois.

Whitt/Krauss Objects of Fine Art, San Diego, California. Also 1995.

1995
Galerie Rob van den Doel, The Hague, The Netherlands.

1994
Laura Larkin Gallery, Del Mar, California. Also 1992.

Bentley Gallery, Scottsdale, Arizona.

Miami Art Fair, Miami, Florida. Also 1993.

The Rachael Collection, Aspen, Colorado.

1993
Chicago International New Art Forms Exposition, Navy Pier, Chicago, Illinois. Also 1992, 1991, 1989.

1985
Gazebo Gallery, Gatlinburg, Tennessee.

The 1985 Ohio Selection Exhibition, Dayton Art Institute, Dayton, Ohio.

Layering; An Art of Time and Space, The Albuquerque Museum, Albuquerque, New Mexico.

Habatat Gallery, Pontiac, Michigan. Also 1983, 1982, 1980.

Sculptural Glass Invitational, Erie Art Museum, Erie, Pennsylvania.

1982
Contemporary Art in Detroit Collections, The Detroit Institute of Arts, Detroit, Michigan.

Invitational Exhibition of Sculptural Glass, Contemporary Artisans Gallery, San Francisco, California. Also 1981.

Glass Art Gallery, Toronto, Canada. Also 1980, 1979.

1981
Art of Glass: Selections from Columbus Collections, Columbus Museum of Art, Columbus, Ohio.

1980
Art in Columbus: 50 Years, State Office Tower, Columbus, Ohio (from the collection of the Columbus Museum of Art and with support from the Greater Columbus Arts Council).

1979
Prospectus: Glass Masters of Two Eras, National Heisey Glass Museum, Newark, Ohio.

Contemporary Art Glass Invitational, D. Erlien Gallery, Milwaukee, Wisconsin.

1978
Limited Editions and Cohen Gallery Invitational, Cohen Gallery, Newton, Massachusetts.

Glass America 1978, Contemporary Art Glass Group, Lever House, New York, New York.

Contemporary Glass in America, Oklahoma Arts Center, Oklahoma City, Oklahoma. Exhibition traveled to the Arkansas Arts Center, Little Rock, Arkansas.

1977
Glassblowers and Stained Glass Makers of Ohio, Mather Gallery, Case Western Reserve University, Cleveland, Ohio.

Contemporary Art Glass Group, New York, New York.

Selected Bibliography

James Yood, "Crystal Logic," in *The Glass Sculpture of Christopher Ries.* Columbus Museum of Art, Columbus, Ohio, 2001, exh. cat.

Katherine Hause, "Composed Light," *SCHOTT information*, No. 96 (2000).

Janice T. Paine, "Clearly Inspired: Contemporary Glass and its Origins," *American Craft* (October/November 1999).

Karen Chambers, *Clearly Inspired: Contemporary Glass and Its Origins.* Tampa Museum of Art, Florida, 1999, exh. cat.

Jeanette Wenig Drake, "Splendor in the Glass," *Alumni Magazine*, The Ohio State University (November 1998).

Henry H. Hawley, *Glass Today: American Studio Glass from Cleveland Collections.* Cleveland Museum of Art, Ohio, 1997, exh. cat.

Steven Kapelke, "Focus: Christopher Ries," *American Craft* (December 1996/January 1997).

Shawn Waggoner, "The Fourth Dimension: The Art Glass of Christopher Ries," *Glass Art* (November/December 1996).

Bergstrom-Mahler Museum, Neenah, Wisconsin, *Crystal Illusions: The Sculpture of Christopher Ries* (1996), exh. bro.

The Everhart Museum, Scranton, Pennsylvania, *Glass & Light: The Sculpture of Christopher Ries* (1996), exh. bro.

Headley-Whitney Museum, Lexington, Kentucky, *Optical Illusions: Glass Sculpture by Christopher Ries* (1995), exh. bro.

Joe Porcelli, "Christopher Ries," PSG's GLASS Artist (April/May 1995).

Richard Briggs, "Windows to a View: The Work of Glass Sculptor Christopher Ries," WVIA-TV, Northeastern Pennsylvania Public Television, Scranton, Pennsylvania (November 1993).

Daniel L. Cusick, "A Clear Look at Christopher Ries," *ArtToday*, Vol. V, No. 3 (1990).

Anita J. Ellis, *Illusions in Glass: The Art of Christopher Ries.* Cincinnati Museum of Art, Ohio 1988, exh. cat.

Mary Polites Smith, "Art is Alive and Well and Living in Columbus: Christopher Ries," *Columbus Homes & Lifestyles* (September/October 1985).

Columbus Museum of Art, Ohio, *Art of Glass: Selections from Columbus Collections* (1981), exh. cat.

Susan Weiss Mulgrew, "A Master in Glass," *Columbus Monthly* (May 1981).

Columbus Museum of Art, Ohio, *Art in Columbus: 50 Years* (1980), exh. cat.

Paul Hotlister, "Glass as Different as Can Be," *Collector Editions Quarterly* (Spring 1979).

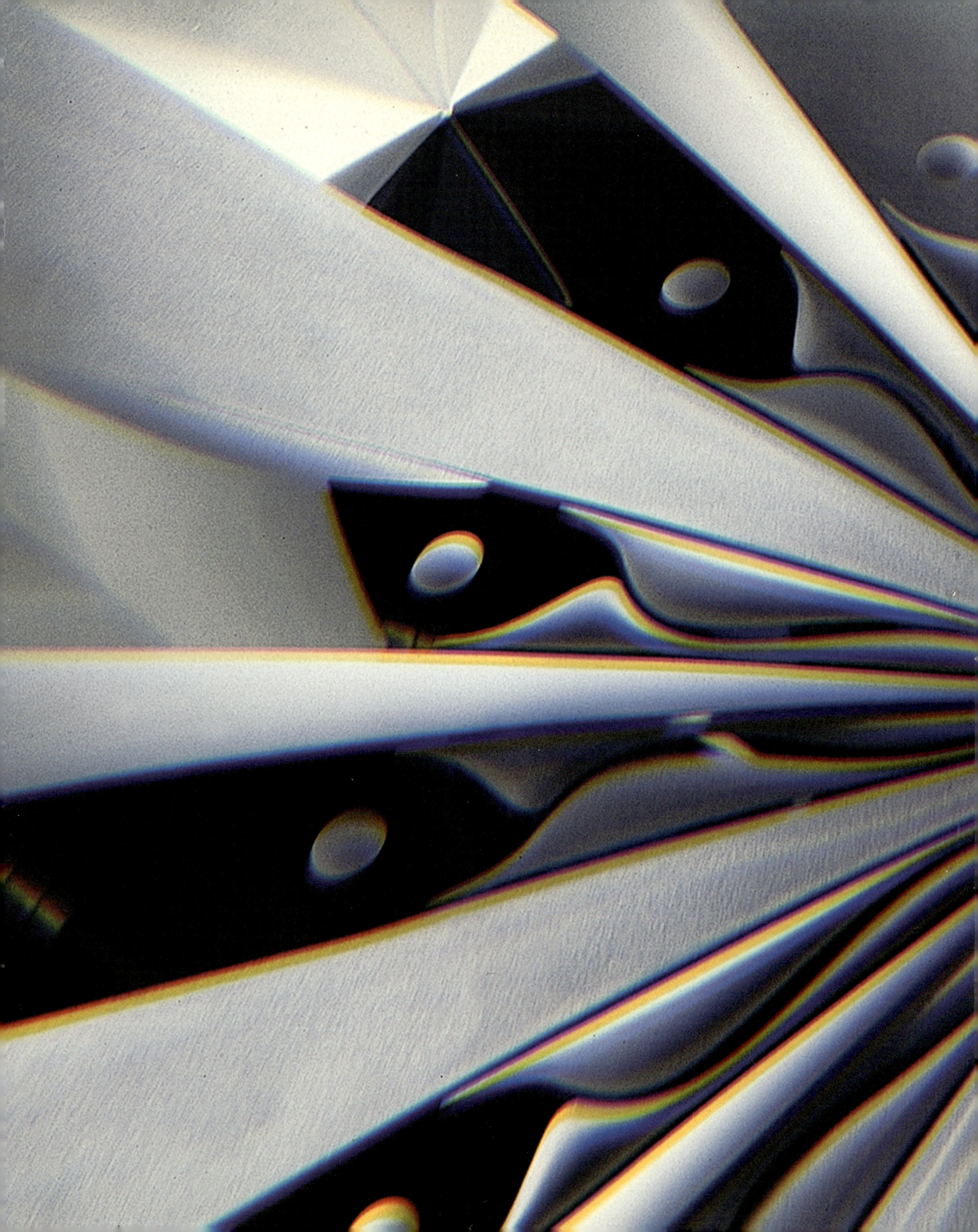